WHAT

Every **1st** Grade Teacher Needs to Know

Margaret Berry Wilson

About Setting Up AND **Running a Classroom**

CENTER FOR RESPONSIVE SCHOOLS, INC.

All net proceeds from the sale of this book support the work of Center for Responsive Schools, Inc., a not-for-profit educational organization and the developer of the *Responsive Classroom*® approach to teaching.

The stories in this book are all based on real events. However, to respect students' privacy, names and many identifying characteristics of students and situations have been changed.

ISBN: 978-1-892989-40-6
Library of Congress Control Number: 2010934764

Cover and book design by Helen Merena
Photographs by Jeff Woodward, and © by Alice Proujansky and Peter Wrenn.

Thanks to the teachers and students of Bronx Charter School for Better Learning, Bronx, New York; Four Corners School, Greenfield, Massachusetts; Hart Magnet School, Stamford, Connecticut; Lincoln Elementary, Harrisburg, Pennsylvania; Sheffield Elementary, Turners Falls, Massachusetts; and Six to Six Magnet School, Bridgeport, Connecticut, who welcomed Center for Responsive Schools to take photos in their classrooms.

Center for Responsive Schools, Inc.
85 Avenue A, P.O. Box 718
Turners Falls, MA 01376-0718

800-360-6332
www.responsiveclassroom.org

Third printing 2017

CONTENTS

Knowing First Graders

First graders often come to school brimming over with enthusiasm and excitement for learning, life, friends, and interests. Theirs is an age commonly marked by tremendous growth, lost teeth, great emotional highs, and, less frequently, some pretty low lows. First graders make big plans, jump into projects with both feet, work at a breakneck pace, and don't want to miss a thing.

My first field trip with first graders was a trip to a local apple orchard. Students examined trees, saw how they were planted, and worked in small groups with parents to pick apples. They all returned with their own small sack. Back at school, we cut apples open and counted seeds in each apple. We compared whether all had the same amount. Some students wanted to plant their seeds, so we quickly rounded up some containers of dirt to do this. With parent volunteers, we proceeded to make miniature apple pies, reading recipes and noting how the apples changed in the cooking process. By the end of the day, the parents and I were completely exhausted but feeling pretty satisfied with all of the activities we had managed to pack in. And then, one first grader piped up: "Is that *it*? What else are we going to do?"

First graders' enthusiasm for school and life can be exhausting but infectious, and teaching them is an exciting and joyful experience (although you *will* need a great deal of energy!). But sometimes first graders' enthusiasm and gusto can make them bite off more than they can chew. They frequently have unrealistic expectations which, when unfulfilled, can crush them with disappointment. (I had to learn to help them realize exactly what we do on field trips before we left to stave off the "Is that it?" disappointment.) Many also experience a great deal of crashing and burning, falling into exhaustion after big spurts of speedy effort.

1

But this is where you come in! You can help first graders realize their grand ideas by breaking the ideas into manageable parts: "You want to write a book about dinosaurs? Okay, let's give each dinosaur you know its own page...." When their plans are a little too grandiose, you can gently bring them back to reality: "I don't think we can have elephants and a circus tent at our end-of-the-year party, but let's think about some other things we could do around a circus theme." You can pace the day so that they don't use up all their energy early and run out of gas for the rest of the day.

I wrote this book to give you strategies for making the most of first graders' common strengths and challenges. You'll find information about many wide-ranging topics, such as scheduling your day, establishing and maintaining a first grade community, handling field trips and other special events, and communicating with parents. Whether you're a new teacher or an experienced teacher switching into first grade, you'll find plenty of strategies and tips in this book to support you and your students.

Begin with Understanding Students' Development

Knowing the students we teach is crucial to being a caring and effective teacher. Even though it's most important to know all the children as individuals—their likes and dislikes, areas of strength, teaching and learning strategies that seem to work best for them—we also need to know generally what to expect from students in this grade so that we can prepare effectively for the year. That means we need to know some of the common characteristics of first graders—for instance, many first graders rush through work, have a competitive streak, and are unduly susceptible to criticism. With this knowledge, we can plan events and assignments that will be engaging and challenging but not overwhelming for them, anticipate which books they'll need in their classroom library, and start the year with appropriate furniture and supplies. Knowing common traits will also give us a place to start if we see or suspect a problem.

First graders' enthusiasm for school and life can be exhausting but infectious, and teaching them is an exciting and joyful experience.

Knowing first graders' unique characteristics also helps immensely in working with parents. For example, first grade parents often worry about how fast their children work. A common refrain is "I don't know why Amy can't slow down. When she does, she's capable of beautiful handwriting, and she doesn't make so many mistakes. Why don't you make her redo all of her work until she learns to take her time?" But parents may find it helpful to know that many first graders share this tendency to rush through work, and most soon grow out of this phase. Because they can also be highly sensitive to criticism, asking them too frequently to redo their work not only tends to have little effect on their speed but also makes them question their abilities. Once parents understand that rushing is typical of many first graders, they are usually more open to suggestions for other ways to help their children balance the tendency to rush with the need for quality standards for school work.

Common Characteristics of First Graders

Of course, first graders have many other characteristics besides being enthusiastic, ambitious, and speedy, and the table on pages 5 and 6 summarizes these other common characteristics. As you use this table, keep these points in mind:

- ■ **Human development is complex.** Even scientists who study it do not yet fully agree on the means by which humans grow socially, emotionally, linguistically, or cognitively. Most theorists describe the process as involving a dynamic interaction between a person's biological disposition and many other environmental factors—including the historical era in which a person grows up, the person's culture and family, and the institutions he or she encounters (such as schools, places of worship, and the media). The table is not intended to ignore this complexity but rather to offer you a bridge between the abstract ideas of theory and their practical expression in children's classroom behavior.

- ■ **Every child is unique.** As a result of the complex and dynamic process of development, no two children—not even identical twins with the same genetic make-up—will develop in the same way or at the same rate. Also, a child may develop much faster in one area than in another. For example, a particular first grader might have social-emotional behaviors very common among first graders (such as bossiness) but cognitive behaviors more like those of a second grader (such as caring about and trying hard to maintain a high standard of work).

■ **The table gives you a practical frame of reference.** For instance, as you will see in the table, many first graders have difficulty staying in their chairs. Teachers who are not aware of this tendency may incorrectly conclude something is wrong with a child who is regularly falling out of his chair. The table is a resource to which you can return if you see a behavior that seems puzzling. You may learn that the behavior is actually fairly common.

■ **The table is not about what's "normal."** It's not intended to limit your thinking about students' potential, to support decisions about whether a student is "normal," or to lead you to ignore the needs of students who differ from other first graders. For example, although many first graders are quite social, talkative, and energetic, you will no doubt encounter quieter, more reserved, and less active students as well. Rather than assuming anything is wrong with these quieter children, think about how you may need to interact with them differently—for instance, by seeking them out more and initiating more conversations with them than with other students. By all means, go with what you see and give students what they need.

To learn more about child development, see the resources in the "About Child Development" section on page 122.

First Graders

Common Characteristics	School Implications

Social-Emotional

■ Are enthusiastic, energetic, and competitive.	■ Provide lots of noncompetitive, cooperative games and activities.
■ Are very social; may start having a best friend.	■ Require students to be quiet only when it's absolutely necessary, and then keep the duration short.
■ Thrive on encouragement and are often crushed by even small criticisms.	■ Reinforce students' positive attributes or behaviors rather than focus on mistakes.
■ Can be bossy.	■ Be understanding of their testing behaviors and bossiness with friends while providing direct guidance and firm limits.
■ May begin to test the limits of authority.	

Physical

■ Are very noisy and active; often fall out of chairs and may need to work standing.	■ Give frequent movement breaks; incorporate movement into the daily curriculum (this helps students stay focused).
■ Can tire easily and get sick frequently.	■ Give students space to spread out their work if possible. Let them work standing up or on the floor.
■ Love playing outdoors and in the gym.	■ Use Interactive Modeling (see pages 38–43) to show students what to do if they fall out of a chair.
■ Are better at tracking from left to right than younger children; this is an ideal age for learning to read.	■ Vary the pace of instruction (quick opening lesson in a circle, back to desks for a focused assignment, return to circle for a discussion) and keep assignments short (5–10 minutes at the beginning of the year).
■ May like to chew on pencils and other objects because new teeth are coming in.	■ Consider having frequent healthy snacks that satisfy students' hunger and chewing urge.

CONTINUED ▶

Common Characteristics	School Implications

Cognitive

■ Are more engaged in process than products.	■ Break activities, assignments, and projects into small, doable chunks.
■ Are very interested in learning and doing "work," but sometimes take on projects that are too big for them.	■ Weave art into as many aspects of the curriculum as possible; provide a wide variety of art materials for exploration.
■ Experience an explosion in artistic interest and expression; love to color and paint.	■ Provide lots of opportunities for imaginative and dramatic play both in the classroom and at recess.
■ Are beginning to be able to conceptualize past and present and cause and effect.	
■ Engage in more elaborate dramatic play.	

Language

■ Love poems, riddles, and songs.	■ Weave poems, riddles, and songs into many parts of the day.
■ Enjoy explaining their thoughts, how something happened, how things work.	■ Provide many opportunities for students to talk and explain their thinking.
■ Ask many questions.	

The information in this chart is based on *Yardsticks: Child and Adolescent Development Ages 4–14*, 4th ed., by Chip Wood (Center for Responsive Schools, 2018), and is consistent with the following sources:

Child Development Guide by the Center for Development of Human Services, SUNY, Buffalo State College. 2002. WWW.BSC-CDHS.ORG/FOSTERPARENTTRAINING/PDFS/CHILDDEVELGUIDE.PDF

"The Child in the Elementary School" by Frederick C. Howe in *Child Study Journal*, Vol. 23, Issue 4. 1993.

Your Child: Emotional, Behavioral, and Cognitive Development from Birth through Preadolescence by AACAP (American Academy of Child and Adolescent Psychiatry) and David Pruitt, MD. Harper Paperbacks. 2000.

6

What About Developmentally Younger and Older First Graders?

Your class will likely contain children with a wide range of chronological ages—children with earlier and later birthdays—as well as children who do not share the common first grade characteristics regardless of where their birthdays fall. These chronologically or developmentally younger students may demonstrate characteristics more like those of kindergartners. Here are some examples of such characteristics and how you might adjust your teaching for these children. Developmentally younger first graders may:

- **Need a great deal of adult approval and like to ask permission.** Give frequent positive reinforcement to all students, check in with students often to make sure they understand directions, and point out students' successes with being independent.

- **Like to repeat experiences and copy previous products.** Reinforce their efforts, but gently nudge them into trying new things and reassure them that mistakes are okay.

- **Struggle with printing.** For instance, they often start in the middle of the line or page, reverse letters and numbers, and space letters and numbers too closely on the page. Provide support and scaffolding for students. You could place dots on the paper to show them where to start writing, give them an object such as a craft stick to mark spaces, or remind them to use their fingers to space between words. It may also help to display examples of good handwriting.

In contrast, some other students in your class might demonstrate characteristics more like those of second graders. These students may:

- **Dislike taking risks and making mistakes.** Present them with new situations and challenges, but prepare them by letting them know what to expect and what strengths they have that they can call upon to overcome the challenges.

- **Like working and playing alone or with one friend.** They may find group work overwhelming. Allow these students to work or sit in pairs as often as possible or provide them with options of quiet places to work.

- **Enjoy one-on-one conversations, especially with adults.** Check in frequently with these students and find time to talk with them at lunch or recess or during other free periods.

- **Try hard to make their work perfect.** Give them shorter, more manageable assignments and help them have more realistic expectations for their work.

How to Use This Book

You can use this book in various ways. For example:

- **Read cover to cover.** If you have time and already know you'll be teaching first grade in the coming year, you may want to read the book from beginning to end to get an overview of how to set up and run the classroom. You may want to take notes or mark key passages to return to later.

- **Right now all I want to know is…** Maybe you're already in the middle of the year, or you just found out that you'll be teaching first grade and you have only a few days to get ready. If you don't have time to read the whole book, zero in on what will help you immediately. Perhaps

a feeling of community is lacking in the room—in that case, go to Chapter 3, "Building Community," on page 57. Or maybe you want to be sure you establish routines and procedures so that the classroom runs smoothly. If so, you could turn to Chapter 2, "Schedules and Routines," on page 33. Read what you need, and then return to the other chapters later when you have more time.

Whichever way you choose, implement the strategies at a pace that feels comfortable for you. Try out the suggestions that best fit your goals and style and that will help you most immediately. Then, as those suggestions become an automatic part of your repertoire, come back to this book and add more ideas and practices. Some things may not work right away, or you may make mistakes—all teachers do, myself included. But remember that those missteps sometimes lead to our best learning, while modeling for students what real learning looks like.

Last Word

I have been teaching so long that some of my earliest first graders have now graduated from college—and at least one has become a teacher herself. Many stay in touch, and I am curious to know what they remember about their first grade year. Most remember the special events we had, learning to read, laughing a great deal, and talking. One student reminded me how he used to begin a conversation with me at lunch and keep talking even when I had to go check on someone else. Another told me how much it meant to him to have the freedom to write frequently about whatever he wanted—and that I responded so positively to his stories even though, looking back on them, he sees that they were somewhat wild, messy, and far-fetched.

These "old" first graders help me keep my eye on what really matters amid the clamor of testing requirements, schedules, and the other day-to-day demands of teaching. Our first graders need us to give them the space to be themselves while still gently nudging them toward growth. They need us to build in the special moments, events, and surprises they crave. They need us to see their strengths and help them build on those. It is an exhilarating year to teach—no one forgets their great first grade teacher!

CHAPTER 1

Classroom Setup

With the high energy and enthusiasm they bring to school, first graders need a classroom that is bright, open, and well organized. They need desks or tables at which to work but also space to move and spread out. They need interesting supplies for the hands-on projects that will engage them. They need to see their work displayed frequently and to feel that the classroom is theirs.

When I set up a first grade classroom for the first time, I made many mistakes. Probably my biggest mistake was overcrowding. At the outset, the room contained twenty-two desks, a large teacher's desk, three different tables I planned to use for centers, and multiple bookshelves. Students were constantly bumping into things and each other. They didn't have room to spread out the way they liked and needed to.

So, one Saturday, I started getting rid of stuff—lots of it. Gone were my teacher's desk and two of the three tables. I moved most shelves against the walls so that we had a larger open space in the center of the room where we could meet together and where students could work if they chose. When the students came back on Monday, we had a fresh start. A new sense of calm infused the classroom, and I was amazed that these small changes to our room could make such a difference.

This chapter aims to help you avoid my mistakes by starting with a classroom setup that will make the most of first graders' energy and enthusiasm. It will advise you on arranging the furniture in your room, acquiring materials, storing and organizing supplies, and making classroom displays meaningful for students.

Arranging the Furniture

Whole-Group Circle

No first grade room would be complete without a space where the children can gather together in a circle. The circle gives socially oriented first graders the sense of community and belonging they crave, which is crucial for setting a positive and happy tone for the day. Because everyone can see and be seen in a circle, first graders receive attention from and feel connections with everyone else in the class. I use the *Responsive Classroom®* Morning Meeting structure to begin each day, but whatever structure you choose to use, the circle area will help your class joyfully begin each day as a community.

It's also important to use the circle area (as well as desks or tables) for academics so that first graders won't have to spend their day in one place. With their energy, they need the change of pace provided by having some lessons in the circle and some lessons at their desks. At a more practical level, activities such as interactive writing, math with manipulatives, and hands-on science and social studies lessons often work better in the circle. Students can also sit on the floor in the circle area for small group work.

Learn More About Morning Meeting at
www.responsiveclassroom.org

The Morning Meeting Book, 2nd ed., by Roxann Kriete and Carol Davis (Center for Responsive Schools, 2014).

Ways to Use the Circle

Curriculum Area	Use the Circle for . . .
Social	Class meetings, practicing social skills and routines, group games and activities
Writing	Mini-lessons, work sharing, interactive writing
Reading	Read-alouds; partner chats about books, poetry, and other shared reading experiences; dramatizations of books; mini-lessons about reading strategies or phonics; independent reading
Math	Explorations of manipulatives, mini-lessons, math games
Social studies	Read-alouds, examination of artifacts, dramatizations of historical and political events
Science	Read-alouds, examination of materials, experiments and other hands-on activities

First graders will spend so much time in the circle that I recommend starting your classroom design there. Key considerations:

■ **Use a large space.** First graders can be clumsy and also like to touch those close to them, so be sure to give each child as large a personal space as possible. The circle space will also need to be big enough for a chart stand and other supplies you'll need for whole-group instruction.

■ **Make an actual circle.** The children need to be able to see everyone else. Other shapes like ovals, squares, or amorphous shapes subtly leave some first graders out. This subtle message will not only cause hurt feelings but may also lead some first graders to find other, less desirable ways to make themselves seen and heard.

■ **Mark spots.** First graders are movers, so having a spot physically marked with tape strips, for example, helps them orient themselves. Without

"I Don't Have Room for a Circle!"

Unfortunately, this is not an unusual dilemma for teachers—even more so in first grade, since these children are generally unable to move desks and furniture efficiently and independently. But there is one possible solution: Use a space outside the classroom as a meeting area.

Go to the cafeteria, library, gym, or other space in the school that's large enough to accommodate a circle. This solution, which is admittedly quite challenging, works best when you:

- **Use the same space every day.** The familiarity will help children succeed.

- **Limit distractions.** For example, if you use the cafeteria, meet when no other class is there.

- **Meet at the same time every day.** Even if it's not the most ideal time, the predictability will help students feel secure and enable them to focus.

- **Teach the expected behaviors.** Be sure to teach and model transition routines and expectations for behavior outside the classroom.

Interactive Modeling

See Chapter 2, "Schedules and Routines," pages 38–43, for a full explanation of Interactive Modeling.

14

The whole-group meeting circle is the heart of classroom life. Sitting in a circle, everyone can see and be seen by everyone else. And because the circle has no beginning and no end, it allows everyone an equal place in the group. By the very nature of its design, the meeting circle invites group participation and fosters inclusion. Its presence and prominence in the classroom or in the school day says, "In this classroom, we value working together, and we value each individual's contributions to the group."

these marked spots, you may spend too much time directing children to back up, move forward, or otherwise readjust the circle.

- **Assign circle seats.** Not only are first graders quite social, but they also tend to be bossy and interested in others' decisions. Left to their own devices, they will not only worry about where they should sit but where their friends should sit as well. Solve this problem by assigning circle seats.

- **Rotate seat assignments.** First graders love to move around and interact with a wide variety of friends. Help them accomplish this by changing their circle seats every week or two.

- **Move children as needed.** Sometimes we think two students will work well next to each other, but they don't. Be ready to move children as needed to make circle time positive and productive.

- **Don't give up.** If your room is small, you may need to get creative in finding space for a circle, but resist the urge to give up on it. Instead, think about whether you can save space in other areas of the room. (See "I Don't Have Room for a Circle!" on the opposite page for another idea.)

Desk Seating

Although the circle is an important whole-group teaching space, first graders also need desks or tables at which to do their independent and cooperative group work.

- **Set up groups.** Arrange desks in groups of four, five, or six, or use tables. Most first graders love being in groups and will work best in this cooperative, open way.

- **Avoid front-facing rows.** This arrangement sets talkative and social first graders up for failure, as they will likely spend much of their time leaning over to chat with others, turning around to see what friends are doing, and falling out of their chairs as they do so.

- **Have stand-up workspaces.** Some first graders work best when standing. Some can stand at their desks. Taller first graders may be more comfortable using the tops of low bookshelves or cabinets, movable TV trays, or other surfaces around the room.

Tips for Assigning Desk Seats

- Balance the number of boys and girls if possible. Make sure all students eventually sit with everyone in the class.

- Group students who have been working well together lately.

- Group children who need lots of quiet.

- Do some children need a little extra help at work time? Have them sit with classmates who will be able to help (without being distracted from their own work).

■ **Offer alternative spaces.** First graders who crave more quiet may find tables of four or more to be challenging. Still others might ordinarily work well in such groups but may occasionally choose to work alone. So scatter a few single or double desks in several different areas. If you don't have room for this, provide clipboards for students. Using the technique of Interactive Modeling (presented in Chapter 2, pages 38–43), show students how it will look if they choose one of these alternate work spaces. Set up the expectation that once students choose an alternate space for a given work period, they should stay there.

■ **Assign seats at tables or desks.** You can avoid the stress, drama, and hurt feelings that sometimes result when first graders choose their own seats by choosing seats for them.

■ **Change desk assignments frequently.** Because of first graders' lively interest in others, it might be a good idea for you to change their desk assignments once every three to five weeks so that students have an opportunity to get to know a wide variety of classmates.

Three Pieces of Furniture You Can Lose

■ **A teacher's desk.** These often take up a great deal of space, but we seldom use them to teach. They tend to become places to store things and sit at the end of the day. When I got rid of my desk, I had many more options for arranging the classroom and collected much less clutter.

■ **A large file cabinet.** These eat up space, too, and encourage us to keep things we don't need. Think smaller. What files are truly essential? You can probably store these in one or two small, mobile file cabinets.

■ **The latest, greatest thing.** Education has fads, and furniture is no exception. My first year of teaching, I paid too much for a nifty folding table to house the listening center. The table never really worked and always seemed to be in the way. You're better off sticking to the basics.

Other Areas of the Classroom

Although it's a good idea to keep furniture and other materials to a minimum, you'll need a few additional areas and furnishings:

■ **A multifunctional table area.** You'll need a separate table of any shape where you can work with small groups on reading, writing, or math. This table could also function as an art area if students have special projects to complete.

■ **A classroom library.** First graders need a wide collection of books at a variety of levels. If possible, store books within easy reach for students and in front-facing baskets so that students can flip through and see the covers as they browse. (See the box, "The Classroom Library," on page 22 for more on classroom books.)

■ **Accessible storage.** Math, social studies, science, and art supplies for students' independent use need to be clearly marked, well organized, and easily accessible to all children.

■ **Private storage.** You'll need your own storage areas, not accessible to children, for all extra supplies, plus the art supplies such as glitter, paint, and fancy paper that you make available only on special occasions.

■ **A computer area.** If you have classroom computers, avoid distractions by giving them their own area. If this is impractical because of space considerations, cover the computers when not in use.

Classroom Supplies

Many first graders are prolific artists, writers, and creators and learn best from hands-on activities and projects. Try to make sure the classroom is stocked with a wide variety of writing supplies, art materials, math manipulatives, and similar supplies. Follow these guidelines for acquiring supplies and helping children use and care for them.

Have Community Supplies Only

Having community supplies that all students share eliminates problems among often-competitive first graders, who may spend considerable time arguing about who has the best pencil or set of markers. This method also ensures that all students have what they need even if their parents can't afford supplies or don't have the time to go get them. And perhaps most importantly, having community supplies conveys a strong message that everyone in the classroom is equal and that learning will be a joint adventure for the year.

Despite all the good reasons for having them, many parents may not be used to community supplies and may not understand their benefits. Be sure to share your reasons for choosing this approach.

18

No Budget for Supplies?

If your school does not give you a supply budget but instead relies on parents to provide supplies, you could replace the traditional shopping list with assignments so that each parent donates one category to the class. For example, one parent supplies the pencils, another some markers, and so forth.

Also, you could explore using a website set up to link interested donors with classrooms:

■ WWW.DONORSCHOOSE.ORG
■ WWW.ADOPTACLASSROOM.ORG

What Supplies Do They Need?

Stocking a first grade classroom can be both exciting and overwhelming. Use the following chart to help you choose the most essential supplies. Focus on the beginning of the year and then add additional supplies as the year goes on. However, you'll only need to purchase many supplies once.

Good Supplies for a First Grade Classroom

Category	Early in the Year	Later in the Year	Sample Quantities
Literacy	■ Books (variety of genres and reading levels) ■ Listening center and audio books ■ Variety of lined and unlined paper ■ Pencils ■ Pencil grips ■ Erasers ■ Writing notebooks, journals, or folders ■ Clipboards ■ Magnetic letters and cookie sheets	■ Books (new genres and authors to replace some books as the year progresses) ■ Bookmaking supplies	■ Pencils—about eight per student ■ Clipboards—one per student ■ Magnetic letters and cookie sheets—enough for a group of four or five children
Math	■ Counters ■ Unifix cubes ■ Pattern blocks ■ Rulers ■ Calculators ■ Variety of math games ■ Dice or spinners ■ Playing and numeral cards with numbers from 1 to 10 (or higher) ■ Real or play coins	■ Tangrams ■ Geoblocks ■ New math games ■ Play clock with movable hands ■ Base ten and attribute blocks	■ Pattern blocks, Unifix cubes, etc.—several sets ■ Rulers and calculators—one per student ■ Playing and numeral cards—one set of each for every two students

CONTINUED ▶

Category	Early in the Year	Later in the Year	Sample Quantities
Art	■ Crayons ■ Colored pencils ■ Markers (thin and thick) ■ Watercolors ■ Drawing paper ■ Construction paper ■ Magazines for cutting and other paper scraps ■ Brown paper bags ■ Found objects (buttons, fabric, cotton balls, etc.) ■ Scissors ■ Glue and glue sticks ■ Tape ■ Modeling clay ■ Craft sticks	■ Paint ■ Colored tissue paper ■ Yarn ■ Glitter ■ Toothpicks ■ Small trays for paint (ask the meat department at your local grocery if you can have some for free) ■ Hole punch ■ Origami paper ■ Stapler	■ Scissors—one pair for every student ■ Glue—one bottle for every two students ■ Glue sticks—two per student ■ Markers, crayons, colored pencils—an ample supply for each table or desk cluster ■ Yarn, glitter, other specialty supplies—bring out less often. Quantity depends on how many students will use these, and how often.
Social studies	■ Globe ■ Maps, especially of school and local area	■ Map puzzles ■ Theme-related artifacts, pictures, and posters	■ One globe per class ■ Maps of different types

Good Supplies for a First Grade Classroom CONTINUED

Category	Early in the Year	Later in the Year	Sample Quantities
Science	■ Hand lenses ■ Small trays (ask the meat department at your local grocery if you can have some for free) ■ Magnets ■ Balances	■ Balance scales ■ Containers for growing things or holding living things ■ Theme-related artifacts, pictures, and posters	■ Hand lens—one for each student ■ Small tray—at least one per student ■ Balance scale—one for every two students
Recess (outdoor and indoor)	■ Variety of balls ■ Hula hoops ■ Jump ropes ■ Sidewalk chalk ■ Bubbles ■ Board games ■ Puzzles	■ More complex games ■ More complex puzzles	■ Three to four balls per class ■ Four to six single jump ropes and two longer ones

See the appendix (pages 113–116) for favorite books, board games, and websites for first graders.

Quality Matters

Having high-quality supplies gives first graders the message that what they do at school is important. Classroom life will also be much smoother if the materials and supplies work well; otherwise, reading and math groups may be interrupted by frequent reports that "This marker isn't working!" Also, if some supplies work well but others do not, students may compete over the limited quality supplies. First graders, who often rate themselves according to who has the most or best, may be motivated to hide good supplies for themselves or may feel the need to brag each time they get the "good scissors."

The Classroom Library

Most first grade classes include students with a range of reading abilities, from those who are reading books with only one or two words per page to those who can read chapter books. So first graders will need a classroom library with many levels and types of books. To get started, consider these categories (for some suggested titles, see the appendix on pages 113–116):

- Emergent or beginning readers at many different levels
- Picture books from simple to complex
- Beginning chapter books
- Poetry collections
- Simple comic books

- Nonfiction books about animals, rocks, the way things work, famous people, etc.
- Children's magazines
- Pop-up books
- Knock-knock joke books (a genre made for first graders!)

If you are starting from scratch, here are some ideas to help you stock up fast:

- Use book clubs (such as Scholastic or Trumpet)—some offer beginning-of-the-year specials or bonus points to get free books
- Scavenge from other teachers—they often have extra copies of books

- Visit garage sales or school book drives
- Ask for parent donations
- Check local library sales

Finally, organize the classroom library to fit first graders. These children often are drawn to books in categories, so organizing them that way (fairy tales, animals, and so on) can be helpful. Don't organize books by reading level, since this public ranking of books often unwittingly fuels the competitive urges of first graders and can lead them to compare themselves with others. You may also want to put a "just right" book in some kind of container for each student to make sure the children read books that are appropriately challenging for them.

Storing and Organizing Supplies

Use an organizational system that will make sense for both you and the students. Some categories of supplies:

- **Desk supplies.** Depending upon your curriculum, first graders may have a variety of notebooks, journals, books, or workbooks to which they need easy access, so you'll want them to keep these things in their desks. Without some guidance from you, though, they may also see their desks as a convenient location for many other objects they find interesting. Make guidelines for what goes in and what stays out of desks, and allow time for regularly keeping personal spaces organized. You can also post a visual of the organization system as a reminder for students.

- **Close-at-hand supplies.** First graders will need some supplies—such as pencils, markers, colored pencils, and crayons—so frequently that it makes sense to have those always within reach. To enhance the community nature of such supplies, keep them in bins or caddies in the center of desk groupings or tables.

- **Other regularly needed supplies.** Because hands-on exploration is so important for first graders, many other supplies should be stored in a place where the children can readily get to them when needed. These might include frequently used art supplies, math manipulatives, or some science supplies. Place these in open or easy-to-open baskets or containers on shelves. Group and label the baskets or containers according to purpose or theme—math materials together, art materials in one place, and so forth.

- **Special supplies.** You may have some supplies for which quantities are limited and others that you want to save for special occasions. Keep such supplies in your own private storage areas, out of the children's sight.

Teaching Students How to Access and Maintain Supplies

Once you have your organizational system down, introduce the supplies. Use extra care when introducing supplies with which students may be less familiar. Teach students about:

■ **Finding supplies.** Make sure students understand exactly where to find each type of material.

■ **When to use supplies.** Let students know how to tell when it's appropriate to access a given area. Using simple "open" or "closed" signs can help.

■ **Caring for supplies.** How do students care for supplies that are in use? Can they mix colors of Play-Doh? How will they keep glue sticks from drying out and paint brushes soft and pliable? Think through care issues and model for students important aspects of caring for supplies. Take photographs of students showing appropriate care with materials and post them near the supply storage area for reference.

More Tips for Supplies

■ **Scrap box.** Have a box or basket in which students can place large unused scraps of paper. First graders love these scraps, and using them teaches thrift.

■ **Pencil sharpener.** Active first graders often see the pencil sharpener as a great energy expender. They find electric pencil sharpeners particularly enticing. Avoid having all your pencils quickly reduced to nubs by providing an extra basket of sharpened pencils and a place for students to put pencils that need sharpening. You can also provide individual, nonelectric sharpeners for students to keep at their desks.

■ **Book return box.** No matter how well you explain the way the books are organized, first graders may have trouble getting books back to the right basket. Creating a "return books here" basket and reshelving books yourself will help keep the classroom library in reasonable working order.

■ **Putting supplies back.** Be explicit in pointing out the labels on the containers and the shelves. Students I've taught sometimes enjoy playing a game called "beat the clock cleanup." Students get baskets from various areas of the room, along with a challenge to put the proper supplies in their baskets and then put the baskets away quickly, safely, and correctly while you keep time.

■ **Keeping insides of desks and storage areas neat.** It helps first graders to have a clear visual of the goal for the inside of their desk (notebooks on bottom, folders next, or however you want things arranged), so post a picture or drawing of an organized desk. Building a brief organizational check time at least twice into the daily schedule and teaching students how to use this time will also keep those unwanted objects and big messes from growing inside students' desks.

Interactive Modeling

See Chapter 2, "Schedules and Routines," pages 38–43, for a full explanation of Interactive Modeling.

■ **Continuing use of supplies.** How will students know if they're on the right track with supplies? First graders respond especially well to positive reinforcement, so be sure to notice and point out when they return supplies in a neat and organized way.

■ **Problems with supplies.** Be sure students know what to do if they encounter problems with supplies. For instance, is it okay for a student to interrupt you during a reading group to report a problem with supplies, or should the student leave you a note or put a tally mark on a supply sheet?

Making Supplies Last

First graders tend to be highly productive and will likely quickly consume every supply you give them. Make the supplies go further by putting out only what students will need for short periods of time. For instance, put out the amount of paper that you think students will need for two weeks. Put out enough markers to last students for a month or two. Let students know if you have additional supplies and when you'll bring them out.

Classroom Displays

Some Guiding Principles

■ **Less is more.** The fewer displays you have up, the more likely that first graders will notice and benefit from them. Conversely, overdoing displays may overstimulate students and may make the room feel jumpy instead of orderly and calm. Aim to have a great deal of open space both on the walls and on the shelves.

■ **Make displays purposeful.** All displays should serve a purpose. Know why you're devoting the time and effort to displays and make sure children understand the point of each display as well (for example, if you show students' work, consider having an "opening day" to discuss each piece). Likewise, let students know how displays such as brainstormed lists or reference charts can help them—if possible, make use of such displays during your mini-lessons or demonstrations. Take down outdated displays or those that you notice children aren't using.

■ **Use only essential text.** Even strong first grade readers can be easily overwhelmed by text-heavy displays. Keep the text on displays brief and large enough for students to see easily.

Put It at Eye Level

Whenever possible, put displays at the children's eye level. First graders generally focus on objects close at hand. They may pay little attention to displays high up on a wall.

Let Student Work Dominate

Most first graders are quite proud of everything they do and get very excited when they see their writing, stories, or other work up on the walls or on the tops of shelves. Such displays also tell students you value their efforts and let classmates and classroom visitors appreciate student creativity. Aim to:

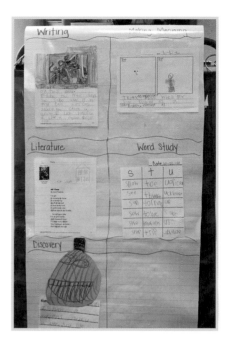

■ **Include everyone.** Display work from everyone in the class, not just the highest-achieving students.

■ **Display finished and draft work.** First graders value finishing so much that including some unfinished pieces will help them realize that a carefully executed but unfinished piece of work has as much value as a completed end product that's less carefully done.

■ **Give students a say.** Allowing student input about what you show makes displays more interesting to them, helps reinforce their efforts, and fosters a feeling of community. Having different displays for each student also encourages individuality and cuts down on first graders' innate competitiveness. One easy way to create and sustain a student work display is to create a bulletin board with one square for each student. Add a small photo of each child to a corner and then let students decide what gets displayed in this space and when it's time to change things.

■ Include photos. First graders love to see pictures of themselves, so when possible, also consider displaying photos of students acting out stories, reading, playing math games, or doing other work that is not recordable with pencil and paper.

■ **Plan for three-dimensional displays.** To help acknowledge the importance of hands-on projects, use the tops of bookshelves or countertops to display students' use of math manipulatives, science experiments or discoveries, and other three-dimensional projects. Photos of these projects will also work if you have limited shelf and countertop space.

■ **Be sensitive to learning differences.** You may not want to display work by students who are struggling in the subject of the display if doing so might cause embarrassment. If you can, take struggling students aside and, one-on-one, help them create a suitable work for display.

Other Displays

■ **Year-long charts.** Some displays, such as a class calendar, birthday graph, or charts that you continually update ("Insects We've Discovered," "Ways We Have Improved," and so on), will be meaningful to first graders all year long, especially if you refer to them regularly. Some maps (such as a school map or one of your town, state, or country) might also prove useful. More rarely, you may want to display some procedural charts— for instance, a list of choices for what students should do when they finish work early. Be sure to use icons for nonreaders and explain and practice how these charts can help. You'll also want to keep classroom rules up all year as a constant reminder of behavior expectations.

■ **Current teaching tools or content.** Displays or charts the children help create as you teach lessons—such as a brainstormed list of writing topics—may also be meaningful. You may also occasionally want to display photos or reference information supporting students' learning in literacy, social studies, and other content areas. But it's easy to overdo these—remember the principles "less is more" and "all displays should serve a purpose." First graders are more likely to use reference materials if they are close by, so consider making desktop versions of alphabet sound cards, spelling lists, and so on (or place them inside students' notebooks or journals).

Technology

Although first graders are more technologically savvy than ever, they will still need your help learning to use technology appropriately in the classroom. Among other things, you'll need to establish when and how they can use technology and what to do if something goes wrong.

To help first graders succeed with computers and other devices:

■ **Model and practice device use.** Show the whole class the steps to follow to access information or software. Make sure students have a chance to practice what you show them so that they can be fairly independent with interactive games and informational sites.

- **Share the devices.** Make sure all students, not just those who finish first or need an extra challenge, get to use computers and other devices. Assign days or time slots, or have a sign-up sheet on which students can choose from a limited number of time slots.

- **Supervise carefully.** Despite your best modeling of how to use technology, students may run into problems, push buttons they shouldn't, or become a bit too adventurous. So be sure an adult is close by and available to supervise when students are using technology. If you're in the room but too far away to see what's on the screens, you may want to restrict students to non-Internet activities.

- **Set boundaries on Internet use.** Know your school's policies about students' Internet usage, what blocks your school has in place, and what websites you're comfortable having students visit. Then teach students these boundaries.

- **Consider accessibility issues.** Work with the experts in your school to ensure that every child can access the technology resources you plan to use.

30

Yes, It's Cool, but Do We Really Need It?

New technology can be so exciting, and we want students to be up-to-date. But if you have a say over what equipment goes into the classroom, exercise caution and put technology in perspective with everything else students need.

Closing Thoughts

The time and thought you put into setting up the classroom and choosing supplies with first graders' needs in mind will pay off all year long. In a logical, well-ordered room, stocked with everything they need, first graders will be able to fulfill their many big ideas without getting overwhelmed. They will be encouraged to expend their boundless energy in positive, productive ways. Of course, you may need to make changes once you get to know students or if you discover that something isn't working, but rest assured that if you pay attention to their needs, students will feel relaxed and confident in the comfortable, planned space you created for them.

CHAPTER 2

Schedules and Routines

An important job of first grade teachers is to create schedules and routines that help first graders pace themselves, organize their energetic and active ideas, and reach the end of the day tired but happy. The first graders I've taught have found the set routines of our day reassuring. Our morning gathering, doing daily equations, singing or reciting poetry together, and all the other predictable routines throughout the day help them maintain both their energy and enthusiasm for school. One year there was a bathroom in our classroom, and I often heard children singing in there as we worked. I always knew the pace and rhythm of our day was just right when I heard as much singing at the end of the day as at the beginning!

33

In this chapter, I'll give you practical ideas for helping first graders make the most of the industriousness they bring to school.

Scheduling

Creating an effective daily schedule for first graders means capitalizing on their energy without letting them wear themselves out—and balancing those considerations with your school's scheduling requirements.

Consider How First Graders Learn Best

First graders are very curious and love the opportunity to explore topics of interest to them, but they also crave the security of having routine, structure, and plenty of time to do their best work.

Consider these needs as you plan your schedule and lessons:

■ **An up-and-down pace to the day.** First graders tend to be active, energetic people, but too many active periods in a row can exhaust them and leave them little energy to last the day. They should have some periods of

sustained, quiet work interspersed with more active periods.

■ **Active, hands-on learning.** Although first graders benefit from some direct teaching and seatwork, make most lessons as active as possible—for instance, choose strategies such as shared reading or interactive writing, use manipulatives for math, and make science and social studies hands-on whenever you can.

■ **Interactive learning.** First graders commonly like to talk, so intersperse lessons and independent work times with opportunities for talking. For instance, if writing time needs to be relatively quiet, allow students to do some talking (possibly through partner chats) during the writing mini-lesson beforehand and the reflection afterward. Even when doing "independent" reading, first graders may need to read aloud quietly to themselves. You might also follow quiet times with a quick song or game that allows for talking and interacting.

■ **Freedom within limits.** First graders often have a lot of creativity and innovation, so try to find ways for them to use these qualities in their work. For example, you could have students create or solve story problems in math through writing, drawing, or using manipulatives. However, some first graders also have a tendency to bite off more than they can chew, so be sure to provide some parameters for more open assignments. For instance, in my classrooms, when

What About Pacing Guides?

Many schools require teachers to follow pacing or time guides. Of course, you'll need to adhere to these, but try not to lose sight of the children's needs in the process. If your district requires ninety minutes of language arts instruction, for example, find out if these have to occur in one block. If not, consider putting math or science in the middle of the block. If the ninety minutes must occur in one block, work in some quick movement activities, talking, hands-on work, or reflection breaks.

For lively movement breaks that take just one to three minutes, see *Energizers! 88 Quick Movement Activities That Refresh and Refocus* by Susan Lattanzi Roser (Center for Responsive Schools, 2009) available at www.responsiveclassroom.org. Other resources are listed in Chapter 4, "Classroom Games, Special Projects, and Field Trips," starting on page 81.

first graders made new versions of children's books we had read, I limited them to two pages a day to make sure they didn't try to rush through and write a "whole book" in half an hour.

★ ■ **Changes of pace and place.** Make sure first graders have ample opportunities to move, change places within the room, and interact with many classmates. For instance, start lessons in the circle, move students to their desks for independent work, and have them return to the circle for reflection. Also keep the pace of lessons fairly quick so that first graders, who sometimes struggle with attentiveness, can stay focused.

■ **Food and water.** First graders need to eat—frequently. When I first started teaching first grade, we had lunch at 10:30 in the morning. I was worried that the children wouldn't be hungry so early and would miss their opportunity to fuel up for the rest of the day. But I discovered that they were very hungry by 10:30 and then again at about 12:30. Try to have periodic snack breaks or a grazing table for those who are frequently hungry. Also, be sure first graders have frequent water breaks.

Do You Need to Do Calendar Time?

Calendar time is a fixture in many first grade classrooms. However, this concept of time, as it's typically used, may not fit most first graders' needs. Children tend to grasp temporal concepts slowly and through experience rather than through rote exercises. They may also be thrown by the use of place value manipulatives to mark the number of days of school and the placing of patterns unrelated to time onto the calendar. Finally, whole-group instruction may not be the best way to teach calendar concepts given the wide range of understanding in most first grade classrooms.

Nonetheless, if you're required or want to do some calendar activities, here are tips for making them purposeful:

■ **Treat calendar time like any other learning block.** Have clear objectives, tie calendar activities to those objectives, and have some way to assess whether children have met the objectives.

■ **Assess children's knowledge.** Make decisions about what to teach at calendar time on the basis of students' knowledge of calendar terminology (days of week, months of year, and so on) and understanding of temporal concepts.

■ **Tie activities to real-life events.** For instance, you could use words or photos to mark events that occurred or are coming up in the classroom. You could then discuss those events in temporal terms such as "last week," "yesterday," or "in two weeks."

■ **Avoid adding too many concepts.** For instance, although first graders do need practice with pattern concepts, try to find ways to practice other than by adding patterns to the calendar.

List the Day's Components

Think about both the academic and social skills learning you want to include in each day. Here are some components I typically list when making a first grade schedule:

Morning meeting
Shared reading
Reading workshop
Chapter book read-aloud
Writing workshop
Word study and spelling
Math

Science
Social studies
Desk organization time
Recess and lunch
Quiet time
Closing routines

Give Movement Breaks Often!

Regardless of what schedule you come up with, insert movement breaks throughout the day as the children need them.

Order the Day

Once you have the parts you'll need to schedule, balance them with your constraints—the class's required lunch time, when their specials are, and so forth. Here are two ideal schedules you could use as a basis for your own:

Two Ideal Schedules

7:45–8:00	Arrival routine
8:00–8:30	Morning meeting
8:30–8:50	Shared reading and reading mini-lesson
8:50–9:50	Reading workshop, including picture book read-aloud or guided reading
9:50–10:00	Snack* (can be combined with quiet reading, listening to jokes/poems, catch-up time)
10:00–10:45	Math
10:45–11:00	Read-aloud
11:00–11:30	Special
11:30–12:00	Recess
12:00–12:30	Lunch
12:30–12:50	Quiet time or desk organization
12:50–1:40	Writing time
1:40–2:00	Word work with snack
2:00–2:45	Science and social studies
2:45–2:50	Desk organization, cleanup, and packup
2:50–3:00	Closing circle
3:00	Dismissal

7:45–8:00	Arrival routine
8:00–8:30	Morning meeting
8:30–9:15	Writing workshop
9:15–9:30	Read-aloud
9:30–9:50	Word work
9:50–10:00	Snack
10:00–10:50	Reading workshop, including picture book read-aloud or guided reading
10:50–11:50	Math
11:50–12:20	Recess
12:20–12:50	Lunch
12:50–1:10	Quiet time or desk organization
1:10–1:50	Science and social studies
1:50–2:00	Snack
2:00–2:30	Special
2:30–2:50	Shared reading and reading mini-lesson
2:50–2:55	Desk organization, cleanup, and packup
2:55–3:00	Closing circle
3:00	Dismissal

*Snack consideration: In some first grades, it works best to have a "grazing station" that students can visit at several designated times of the day. If you choose this option, you won't need a separate snack time.

Teaching Classroom Routines

For teachers, phrases such as "line up," "come to the circle," and "clean out your desk" immediately conjure up specific mental images. But first graders, who often have only a year's worth of school experience, don't always have the same images. One of the key lessons I've learned as a teacher is that I cannot assume students know anything about how classroom routines should look and sound, so I need to deliberately teach them.

Use Interactive Modeling to Teach Routines

Interactive Modeling is a simple but powerful way to help students picture and practice our expectations for certain times and routines of the day. There are seven steps to Interactive Modeling, illustrated by the example on the next page of teaching first graders how to clean up and come to the circle quickly and quietly.

Interactive Modeling: Cleaning Up and Coming to Circle

Steps to Follow	Might Sound/Look Like
1 Say what you will model and why.	"When I give you directions to clean up and come to the meeting circle, we need to do that quickly and safely. Watch while I show you how to do that."
2 Model the behavior.	Ask a student to play the role of the teacher. Go to a student's desk and clean up materials in a safe manner, push in the chair, walk safely but briskly to the meeting circle, and sit calmly while looking at the "teacher." Remain quiet. You do not need to narrate as you model.
3 Ask students what they noticed.	"What did you notice about how I came to the circle?" (If necessary, follow up with questions such as "What did you notice my hands doing?" or "How did I get to the circle?" to prompt children to list the important elements: cleaning up quickly, walking safely, remaining quiet, and so on.)
4 Invite one or more students to model.	"Who can show us how to come to the meeting circle the same way I did?"
5 Again, ask students what they noticed.	"What did you notice about the way Kiana came to the circle?" The children name Kiana's specific safe and focused behaviors.
6 Have all students practice.	"Now we're all going to practice coming to the circle quickly and safely. I'll be watching and seeing you do all the things we just noticed."
7 Provide feedback.	"You did it! You all cleaned up neatly and quickly, you walked directly to the circle, not too slow and not too fast, and you sat down quickly and quietly. We are now ready for a great book."

Keys to Successful Interactive Modeling

BE CLEAR ABOUT HOW YOU WANT THINGS DONE

For example, if you want students to give you a signal to go to the bathroom and wait for your nodding reply, show them exactly what that looks like. Be sure to stick to whatever signal you choose—first graders will be quick to point out if you don't follow your own methods!

> **More Benefits of Interactive Modeling**
>
> Students . . .
>
> - Have opportunities to talk and participate during the lesson—crucial for first graders!
>
> - Become better observers (a skill that transfers into their academic work)
>
> - Begin to value each other as models, which helps build a sense of community and trust
>
> - Become more engaged in monitoring their own behavior

USE A SCRIPT

Having a basic script handy will help you be exact in your modeling—and refrain from talking too much. Using fewer words helps students concentrate on essentials and also allows more time for them to practice and observe.

PRACTICE BEFOREHAND IF NECESSARY

If you need to model lining up, greeting another person, or some other routine that requires student assistants, take a few minutes in the morning (or during other free time) to quickly practice with those students what you expect them to do during the modeling. With a flair for drama, first graders may not always demonstrate behaviors during modeling in the way you would like if they don't have some time to practice first.

KEEP EXPECTATIONS HIGH

Students may need some time during the first weeks of school to practice certain behaviors—we can't expect perfection right away. But once they have a procedure down, be sure to hold them to it. For instance, if you model lining up in an L-shape to accommodate your room set-up, be sure that is how students line up every time. Otherwise, students will be confused or tempted to test limits, or they'll complain to you about how "So and so is not doing it like you said!"

Making Adjustments for Particular Students

Having high expectations is important, but so is recognizing individual needs. Occasionally, you may need to modify expectations for certain students. You may model how to make eye contact when greeting another person, but some children (especially those with diagnoses of autism) are not ready to do this. Some students also may have been taught that making eye contact is not appropriate in their culture. Modify the expectation as needed (for instance, by teaching them to look toward the person or at her forehead). Be sure to discuss with the class why you might occasionally modify rules for particular students. First graders are capable of great empathy when they understand the reasons for changed expectations. Let students know that each of us needs different things to do our best work and that it's the teacher's job to help figure out what each student needs.

KEEP EXPECTATIONS APPROPRIATE

If you're going to expect students to live up to your expectations, it's important to be sure those expectations are appropriate and to take into account the common characteristics of first graders. Knowing that first graders often need to spread out or stand up as they work, be sure to model independent work in several ways, not just sitting at a desk with materials neatly arranged. Because first graders are generally quite talkative and love to move, don't expect silence or even quiet voices when students are eating in the cafeteria. Inappropriate expectations set first graders up for failure, and they can be quite hard on themselves if they "mess up." Think about how to establish routines and model behaviors so that most first graders can and will succeed most of the time.

GIVE STUDENTS PLENTY OF PRACTICE

Students need to practice how to show they're paying attention, how to roll the glue stick down, and how to stop talking when you give them a signal, just as they need to practice reading, counting, and other academic tasks. Set your first

graders up to succeed by giving them practice sessions where they can try out new behaviors and quickly correct any mistakes.

First graders will respond best if the practice is fun, fast-paced, and positive. For example, when practicing how to clean up, push in chairs, and come quickly and safely to the circle, pretend to be the students' "coach." (Wear coach props if you're up for it!) Use a stopwatch and cheer them on as they conclude each step of the process—"Desks are looking clear," "All chairs are in," "People are walking safely—look at our team!" If someone makes a mistake (for instance, forgetting to push in a chair), go over and in your best coach voice, say "_____, I know you can do it—get that chair pushed in!" When all students arrive at the circle, let them know how much time they took. Have a great book waiting for everyone. Practice shouldn't feel like drudgery but like an important and engaging step in becoming a successful classroom community.

SCAFFOLD

If Interactive Modeling seems problematic or students just don't seem to "get it," it may be because you've given too many instructions at one time. So, before using Interactive Modeling, analyze each step involved in the task and look for ways to scaffold by modeling each step separately and then giving appropriate directions. For instance, if students struggle with the transition from working at desks to sitting in the circle, direct them first to clean up. Then, direct them to push in chairs. Then, invite them to the circle.

REINFORCE SUCCESS OFTEN

When things in our classrooms are going well and students are doing routines as we taught them, we sometimes just breathe a sigh of relief and move on to the next thing on our long to-do list. But all students, first graders especially, need us to keep paying attention to what they're doing well. Use specific, direct language that reinforces what you taught in the first

42

place: "I noticed that everyone lined up quickly today and left enough space between themselves and the next person." "While you were in music class, I did a quick check of your desks, and they all look like our picture!" "You all got quiet in about two seconds; I think that may be our fastest time yet." First graders love this positive feedback, and giving it often will keep the lessons of Interactive Modeling alive.

Learn More About Positive Teacher Language
at www.responsiveclassroom.org

The Power of Our Words: Teacher Language That Helps Children Learn, 2nd ed., by Paula Denton, EdD (Center for Responsive Schools, 2014).

If you have a class that generally struggles with routines but a few students consistently do what is expected, be sure privately to recognize their accomplishments. On the other hand, if a few students are struggling, pay particular attention to these students. Think about what they need to succeed (extra practice, modified expectations, closer proximity to you?) and provide it. Look for growth rather than perfection in struggling students. If a student often calls out or interrupts but is slowly beginning to raise his hand or wait to be recognized in some other way, be sure to note that success.

43

Key Routines to Teach

RESPONDING TO SIGNALS FOR ATTENTION

Very little learning can happen in first grade unless you can quickly and efficiently get students to stop what they're doing and pay attention to you, so you'll need to teach effective signals for quiet and attention.

The signal can take many forms—auditory or visual—but students respond best to calming signals like the peaceful sound of a gentle chime or the silent signal of a teacher holding up her

Pitfalls When Using Signals

■ **Speaking before everyone is quiet.** Sends the message that not everyone has to respond to the signal.

■ **Inconsistency in using established signals.** If you say you're going to use a signal but then fail to do so consistently, children may become confused: Is the signal important or not? Do you really mean what you say and say what you mean?

■ **Repeating or using more than one signal.** Teaches students that they don't have to comply right away—they can wait for the second (or third) signal.

■ **Demanding immediate silence.** Can feel disrespectful and may be unrealistic: Students have a natural need to get to a stopping point in their conversation or work (ten to fifteen seconds should do it).

■ **Saying "I'll wait until . . ."** Telling students that "I'll just wait until everyone is ready" gives them the message that they don't have to respond in a timely way and can take as long as they like.

■ **Modeling the "wrong way."** Creates a competing mental picture that will confuse students.

44

hand. Such signals will be much more likely to gain students' attention than the alternatives. Yelling or trying to speak over children's voices often riles them up and can feel quite disrespectful. Starting to speak before everyone is listening implies that only those who are silent have to pay attention. Using a signal effectively provides a clear message that in the classroom, everyone is expected to pay attention, listen to whatever is being said, and learn.

In general, I use two kinds of signals: visual and auditory.

■ **Visual signal.** When they're sitting in a circle or are close to you, students respond quickly and well to a physical gesture. I usually raise one hand high and put the fingers of my other hand over my lips. Children who see this gesture stop what they're doing, become quiet, and copy the signal. Having something to do with both hands helps first graders get needed control over their active bodies, and covering their lips is a helpful reminder to refrain from talking.

■ **Auditory signal.** You'll need an auditory signal to gain students' attention when they are not close to you or are unlikely to see your raised hand. You can use any means of making a calming sound—a chime, a rain stick, or any other instrument with a pleasing tone. Use Interactive Modeling to show students what to do when they hear the sound: stop what they're doing, put all materials down, stop talking, and look at you. Because first graders might be in a variety of places or doing different activities when you use the auditory signal, be sure to practice several of these situations.

Students will also need to gain your attention. Teaching them some simple, nonverbal cues is an effective way to keep the classroom running smoothly and can prevent loud and expressive first graders from interrupting the flow of group lessons.

■ **Taking a turn to speak in a whole group.** When students need your attention in a whole-group situation, they could raise their hand or make a question mark signal. Be clear with students that they should not do this while someone else is talking but should instead wait for a lull or pause in the conversation. This ensures that speakers have everyone's undivided attention and encourages children to listen fully.

■ **"I need to go to the bathroom."** First graders need to go the bathroom frequently. Teach them a signal for letting you know that they need to go and show them what your response will look like.

■ **"I feel fidgety."** When it comes to paying attention, first graders arrive in our classrooms with a wide range of abilities. Some may need an occasional stretch much earlier than others, and you'll want to provide for this without interrupting your lesson or having a student disrupt it. Teach students a signal for "I feel fidgety" or

---

Having a Substitute Teacher? Keep the Schedule and Key Routines in Place!

Schedules. It may be tempting to plan something different to make the day with the substitute, or "guest teacher," feel more special. But first graders will already feel energized and excited by having a substitute—adding changes to the schedule may push that energy level too high.

Routines. Be specific in your lesson plans about any special routines or traditions the class has. For instance, if you typically begin math with a warm-up activity, choose an easy one for the guest teacher, but do not have her skip it.

Other ways to help the day go smoothly:

■ Choose several students whom the guest teacher can ask about the schedule and routines (rotate among students over the course of the year).

■ Discuss with the class ways they can care for one another and the guest teacher while you're out (do what the guest teacher says even if it's different from what you would do, remember that you'll be back tomorrow, and so on). Leave these ideas for the guest teacher to review with the class.

■ Use interactive modeling to teach how to be with a guest teacher. For example, have a colleague, pretending to be the guest teacher, act out doing spelling activities in the wrong order. Model and then let students practice how to do the activities in that order or how to respectfully let her know the correct order.

45

"I need to stretch," such as raising their hand and wiggling their fingers. On your nod, they can get up, stand back from the circle or their desk, stretch, and then return to sitting. Of course, be careful not to let students overuse these signals.

■ **SOS for emergencies.** Teach students a separate signal to use if they or someone near them has an emergency. Be sure to define what an emergency is—a bloody nose, feeling sick, bathroom accident, and so forth—as this is not a natural concept for first graders. An SOS signal—hand shut, hand open, hand shut—works well.

BATHROOM ROUTINES

Be sure to model and practice toilet paper usage, washing hands afterwards, wiping around the sinks, and returning straight to the classroom. Because first graders need to go to the bathroom so frequently, bathroom routines should be among the very first ones you teach.

Given the wide range of bladder control first graders will have, it's unrealistic to think that all of them will be able to hold it until the appointed times of day. If bathrooms are located close to or within your classroom, teach students to use the signal, wait for your okay, and go quickly and quietly on their own. If bathrooms are farther away, teach children to use the signal, wait for your okay, and get a bathroom buddy to go with them. You may want to partner up same-gender students as regular bathroom buddies and use Interactive Modeling to show buddies how to walk with their classmates to the bathroom, wait for them quietly outside, and then walk back to the classroom. Be sure to switch buddies occasionally.

Make a system for students to indicate who's in the bathroom so you won't have to keep track mentally. You could use a pocket chart of all students' name cards and a separate pocket chart with boys' and girls' bathroom slots.

When they need to go to the bathroom, students move their cards to the appropriate bathroom slot and move their cards back when they return. Or, upon receiving your okay signal, students could just get a designated bathroom pass and place it on their desk. When they come back, they return the pass to its storage spot.

Even with the best systems, teaching, and practice, bathroom accidents still occasionally happen in first grade. Store extra pairs of clean underwear and multipurpose pants in a variety of sizes, or have each child keep an extra set of clothes at school, depending on school policy. Accidents happen for a variety of reasons—but if a child has multiple incidents, contact the family to discuss what might be going on.

Also take the time to teach, model, and practice what to do if someone has an accident. Begin by asking students to quietly think about whether they have ever experienced having an accident and how that feels. Ask them to brainstorm how they can take care of classmates should it happen at school (for example, just keep working, go get a teacher, and use kind words). Model and practice what a few of their suggestions would look and sound like. Be ready to take the whole class to the bathroom after this discussion, as it will prompt a need to go!

MORNING ROUTINES

Most first graders enter the day with a great deal of excitement, energy, and enthusiasm, and having a consistent, smooth morning routine will help them channel that energy in positive ways. Some things to consider in planning your morning routine:

- ■ **Check-in.** First graders are often excited to tell you what they've done since they last saw you. If your students enter a few at a time, you can simply greet them and ask them for one piece of news. If many of your students arrive at once, set up a check-in system. For instance, you can announce that you'll be coming around at a certain time to check with each person and hear one thing she or he wants to tell you.

How to Teach Line and Hallway Routines

- **Decide where the line should be.** Where should children line up in the classroom before they leave? Choose a spot with few distractions where all the students can comfortably stand in a line.

- **Teach exactly how to line up.** Model and have students practice walking quickly to the line without stopping to touch or look at anything on the way, facing front, keeping arms at their sides, and leaving space between people (I show students a distance of elbow to fingertips when I model lining up, and they come up with their own way of describing this distance).

- **Teach expected hallway behavior.** If you have a choice, allow children to talk quietly as they walk, as this is more appropriate for first graders. But be sure to model and have students practice exactly what volume is okay. Otherwise, you may end up spending too much time turning down the volume. I also model and have students practice walking at a steady pace and staying together (by maintaining that elbow-to-fingertip distance).

- **Walk with your class.** First graders are not ready for the responsibility of walking as a class without their teacher. They will feel unsafe doing so.

- **Individual activities.** If you have a staggered arrival time, give students something to do (for example, browsing through books, practicing handwriting, using math manipulatives at their desks, drawing, and writing on dry erase boards) while they're waiting for everyone to arrive or for the official morning routine to start.

- **Handing in items.** Show students where and how to hand in notes from home, homework, or needed paperwork.

SITTING IN THE CIRCLE FOR WHOLE-GROUP LESSONS

Be explicit with students about what it looks and sounds like to pay attention while in a whole-group circle and why this matters. Show them how to sit up straight and what to do with their legs—having the options of sitting cross-legged, with legs out, or on their knees generally addresses most first graders' needs. Show students where to put their hands—in laps or on legs—and how to direct their eyes and bodies toward the person speaking.

As the year goes on, you may also want to show them other accepted forms of showing listening, such as smiling or nodding at a speaker or demonstrating a personal connection to what someone else is saying by holding a thumb up.

TRANSITIONS

Although at first, getting a group of first graders to make transitions within and outside of the classroom might seem impossibly chaotic, careful teaching of transitions can make this task simpler. Think through transitions so that you can make them as simple and obstacle-free as possible. Then, break down what students need to do into parts, practice those parts, coach students through them, and focus on quick, efficient uses of time. Fast-paced transitions work well with first graders' enthusiasm and energy.

Transitions into and outside of the classroom:

- **Bringing classroom work to a peaceful close.** Before lining up and leaving the room, give students enough time to clean up their spaces quickly and become calm and quiet wherever they are. You can set a visible timer for this, play a short piece of calming music, or sing a little song together. When the timer goes off or the song ends, all students should be quiet and looking at you, ready to line up.

- **Line tasks.** In line, have students take a deep breath and then give them something to think about as they get ready to leave. ("Start counting by fives—you can whisper in my ear how high you've gotten as you walk out the door.")

- **Returning to the classroom.** Always have the same expectation of what students should do when they re-enter the room—for instance, you could always have them go straight to the circle and direct their attention to a certain spot where you have a preview of your lesson. Another thing that helps first graders is stopping the line outside the door to make sure they are calm and quiet and to reinforce a positive behavior you observed: "Everyone was safe, stayed together, and walked quickly to get here. You are ready for the great math lesson I have planned for this afternoon! Direct your attention to the stand, and I'll see you in the circle."

First, Last, Best? It Matters to First Graders!

With their zest for life and competitive natures, first graders often care a great deal about things such as who gets to be first and last in line, who gets to hand out the papers, or who gets to take some papers to the office. Have a system in place for assigning these responsibilities in a fair way and explain the system to first graders. Some systems you might use include:

- **A job chart.** Assign each student a job for the day or week. Jobs might include line leader, door holder, plant waterer, and so forth. You could make a pocket chart with one pocket representing each job and just move students' cards from one job to the next as needed.

- **Drawing names.** Draw names out of a box or bag to see who does a particular job at a given time.

- **Groupings.** Call students to line up by table groups or categories.

Transitions within the classroom:

■ **Moving from the circle to independent work spots.** First graders need to have a clear picture of how to move quickly and quietly to wherever they're going to work. Model and practice how it looks and sounds for children to leave the circle, get the materials they need, choose a spot to work, and quickly get started. Be ready to stop the group and start over as soon as things go awry in a practice session. Even when students have gotten the transition down, avoid jumping immediately into your own work with small groups or individuals. Instead, stand back and watch transitions to make sure students are doing what they need to quickly and calmly.

50

■ **Moving back to the circle.** Make sure students know how to clean up and return to the circle just as quickly as they left it. Some things students will need to know: where to put materials, what they should do with both finished and unfinished work, what path to take to return to the circle, and how long cleanup should be. Consider playing or singing a song or using a visible timer to help guide this transition.

INDEPENDENT WORK-TIME ROUTINES

No matter what reading or math approach you use, you'll need to model and practice with students how to work independently. Doing work independently may be very difficult for many first graders, but this task is worth modeling and reinforcing. Once students master these expectations, you'll be able to meet with individuals and small groups with few interruptions during independent work time. Some key points:

■ **Talking and noise level.** First graders have a hard time working in complete silence and even do better with some socializing. On the other hand, if they're too loud or too talkative, they won't be able to concentrate and you won't be able to work with an individual or group. Model and practice what an acceptable noise level sounds like. After modeling "some quiet talking," have a small group practice while the rest of the class watches and names the helpful behaviors they saw.

■ **Staying in one place.** Although first graders may need a variety of different spots in which to work, they also need to be productive. Model and practice what it looks like to get all the materials needed and then stay in one spot to complete the task at hand. At the beginning of first grade, expect students to be able to sustain attention for five to ten minutes. Gradually, increase the expectation up to twenty-five minutes.

■ **What to do if they're "stuck."** Model and practice ways for children to get help without interrupting your individual or small group work. For instance, teach them how to seek help from classmates and how to give help when asked. Also have some alternate assignments ready for first graders to work on if friends cannot help (for example, read from a book bin, do an activity with spelling words, or write in a journal). Let students know that in between small group or individual work, you'll come around to see if anyone needs individual help.

■ **Scaffolded independent work-time practice.** After you've modeled independent work time, let students practice with you close at hand—don't immediately begin working with small groups. Once most students seem to have the independent work routine down, remove yourself from close proximity by working with a small group, but give this group fairly easy work to accomplish so that you can really keep your eyes on and give feedback to the "independent" workers. Scaffolding the teaching of independent work in this way will help students find success with it.

READ-ALOUD ROUTINES

It is a joy to read books to first graders! They often take an active and loud interest in what they hear and seem suspended in that magical place where they're still not quite sure what is real and what is fantasy.

Read-alouds with first graders should be as interactive as possible—choose books with lines they can repeat or say along with you such as Mem Fox's *Hattie and the Fox*, Karen Beaumont's *I Ain't Gonna Paint No More!*, or Doreen Cronin's *Click, Clack, Moo: Cows That Type*. First graders also love books with a little suspense, clever plot twists, or surprise endings—first graders I've taught have loved Janet Stevens' *Tops & Bottoms* and Remy Charlip's *Fortunately*.

Follow these guidelines when reading aloud to your first graders:

- **Tell students what kind of book you're about to read.** Be sure to let them know if the book has some lines they can say with you or questions they can call out the answer to, or if the book calls for other responses. If you're reading a less interactive selection, such as a chapter from a chapter book, and want more quiet participation, let students know this as well.

- **Schedule effectively.** Read aloud throughout the day. To ensure that students get the most out of read-aloud time, try to schedule read-alouds after students have had a chance to move or have just sat down—for instance, right after a transition, when they return to the classroom from PE, or after a quick energizer or movement break. You could read knock-knock jokes and silly riddles as students are arriving at the circle area or getting ready to leave the classroom. Keep your introduction to read-alouds quick and purposeful so that most of first graders' attention and energy can go into following the reading selection itself.

Remember to Teach Recess and Lunch Routines!

See Chapter 3, "Building Community," starting on page 57, to learn about these middle-of-the-day routines.

- **Scaffold for success.** Set students up for success with read-alouds by beginning the year with simpler, quicker-to-read books that call for more active participation. Gradually increase length and complexity and add longer chapter books—for these, look not only for plot twists and suspense, but also for humor and lovable characters. (Kate DiCamillo's *Mercy Watson* series is a good place to start as a first chapter book read-aloud, and you can move to more complex books such as Dick King-Smith's *A Mouse Called Wolf.*)

EMERGENCY ROUTINES

Students need to know how to take care of themselves and each other during classroom emergencies. Teach children what you expect them to do when "disasters" such as the following occur: someone has a temper tantrum, gets a bloody nose, or throws up. Signal verbally ("This is an emergency time") or nonverbally (use your auditory signal and show the SOS sign) and make sure students take these steps:

- **Students keep working.** If they're working independently, just keep working.

- **Students read at their seats.** If they're meeting in the circle, they return to their desks, pull out a book, and start reading.

Making sure students have mastered this routine will give you the space to take care of the occasional emergency or manage a child's extreme needs quickly and efficiently.

DISMISSAL ROUTINES

Think through exactly what students need to do so that the room is in reasonably good shape, all their belongings are packed up, and they're ready to leave safely and calmly. Try to limit the tasks that need to be completed to as few as possible. For instance, students could complete a desk or cubby check. Then they could get their backpacks, coats, and hats and hang those on the back of their seats. After closing circle, they could go get things from their seat backs and line up for dismissal.

> **Learn More About Schedules and Routines**
> at www.responsiveclassroom.org
>
> *The First Six Weeks of School*, 2nd ed., from *Responsive Classroom* (Center for Responsive Schools, 2015.)

If possible, choose a time earlier in the day to pack homework, papers, and other things that need to go home so that first graders don't need to do this task when they're tired at the end of the day. During the first few days of school, it may help to practice this routine early in the day when first graders' attention and energy are at their highest. Later in the first week of school, carve out a little time to make sure dismissal procedures are done well and effectively.

Learn More About Closing Circles at
www.responsiveclassroom.org

Closing Circles: 50 Activities for Ending the Day in a Positive Way by Dana Januszka and Kristen Vincent (Center for Responsive Schools, 2012).

In addition to the nitty-gritty parts of dismissal, leave a short time for a quick closing circle. Sing a fun song together, do a silent energizer, or reflect on the day's positives ("What kind thing did you do today?" or "How did we follow our rules?").

OTHER ROUTINES

Some other routines and social skills you may want to model and practice:

- Indoor recess routines

- Taking care of and putting away class supplies

- Winning and losing a game graciously

- Fire, earthquake, or tornado drill routines

- Greeting former teachers, friends, and family when you see them around the school

- Completing class jobs

- Closing circle

Closing Thoughts

First graders thrive when their day is well paced and takes into account their need for conversation and movement, their energy and excitement levels, and their need to eat and drink frequently. They also do best when they know exactly what their teachers expect, and they're delighted when their teachers notice that they've met these expectations. Establishing routines and expectations is worthwhile work, as first graders who know what to do and how to do it can be as busy and productive as they love to be.

CHAPTER 3

Building Community

First graders tend naturally to have many of the ingredients of a strong community—they are typically social beings who love to talk and communicate and enjoy being active and doing things with other people. But some of their other traits can work against a feeling of community—they can sometimes be competitive; many enjoy directing other people but do not enjoy being bossed around themselves; and still others become a little too enmeshed in others' "business."

Fortunately, with your skilled guidance, first graders can come together and form a strong bond of community. Through their bond, they'll feel the positive energy and support from their teachers and classmates that will help them thrive in such an important academic year.

It is so satisfying to see how a strong sense of community can help first graders develop empathy, resilience, and many other social skills. One year, my first graders returned to class from art with one of their classmates in tears. While they were outside painting, a high school student had made fun of the child's painting. I was so touched by the care his classmates took of him—they had shepherded him back to class and already had several ideas about how to take care of the problem.

We settled on asking to meet with the head of the high school so a small group of students could discuss the incident. The offended student also decided to write a letter to the high school newspaper to describe what happened and why it was such a problem. (I will never forget my favorite line in the letter: "In the fewcher, I would like it if you would say nice things or nuthing.") The students clearly felt that an insult to one was an insult to all. Such a powerful sense of community can lead to much safer, happier, and productive learning days for first graders. In this chapter, I offer some ideas for how you can build the sense of community and trust that first graders need to help them take care of one another.

Teacher Tone and Demeanor

Teachers are powerful models for students. Every word we say and action we take can show students what it looks like to care for everyone in the classroom, even those who struggle, are different, or are not yet under-stood. We need to start by having a positive tone and demeanor and by showing students what respect, care, and empathy are like in day-to-day life. First graders are always watching us, whether they seem to be or not. Specific ways to model positive behaviors include:

> **Use Your Normal Tone and Cadence When Speaking to First Graders**
>
> We should talk to first graders using the same tone and cadence we would use with adults. Talking in a singsong cadence or high-pitched tone unwittingly gives the impression that we see first graders as pets or as incompetent people. Also, avoid talking about students or letting others discuss students in their presence as if they were not there.

- **Treat everyone with respect.** Use an even, kind, and respectful tone with everyone, even when giving redirections or consequences for inappropriate behavior. If students hear us being harsh or sarcastic with their classmates, they understandably may do that, too.

- **Get to know each child.** Learn about each child's interests, hobbies, family, and likes and dislikes. The more we know about our students, the better we can plan community-building activities that will appeal to all. Getting to know everyone also demonstrates a powerful message of equality and significance to all students.

- **Avoid comparative language.** Many first graders are beginning to categorize and rank those around them—who is smarter or faster or has the most friends. Instead of using comparative language, which feeds into this hierarchical view of the world, use more inclusive language such as "Who has another idea?" or "Let's all work hard on our stories today."

- **Demonstrate empathy and compassion.** First graders often pay particular attention to mistakes—both theirs and others'. Of course, mistakes are natural parts of life and learning. Model empathy when things go wrong by responding calmly. Without criticizing, help children correct their mistakes.

- **Speak about the class as a whole.** Be sure to convey in the way you address the class that they are a unit: "First graders—you showed such teamwork at math today! You were helping each other and following rules for games, and you put away the materials correctly in less than a minute!"

Greetings

First graders love to hear and see their names, and one way to ensure a community feeling in your classroom is to help your students learn each other's names and greet each other in warm, friendly ways.

Set the tone for warm, friendly greetings by personally greeting each child as he or she enters the classroom each day. Sit on a low chair so that you'll be at or near the children's eye level.

Also set up structures for students to learn to greet each other. For example, begin each day in a circle and lead students in a class greeting. Greeting formats could range from children passing a friendly "Hello, _____ [classmate's name]" around the circle to doing a group chant that involves naming every classmate. (See "Good Greetings in First Grade" on page 62 for ideas.) The daily routine of a greeting helps each child feel known and significant, a key step in forming a community.

Ideas for Learning Names

Many first graders learn best in playful, active ways, and the process of learning names is no different. Just be sure that whatever idea you use honors the name that students prefer to be called by (first name? middle name? nickname?) and its proper pronunciation (seek parental help if you need to).

- **Display of students' names.** If possible, have ready a display of everyone's names on the first day of school. Build games and activities into the first few days of school so that students learn each other's names.

- **Simple name games.** Play a game of Who Stole the Cookie from the Cookie Jar? or an I Spy game. Or create a Concentration game using photos and names and play the game as a whole group or as a center activity.

- **Personalized name tags.** Have students decorate name tags to wear and place on their desks and cubbies so that their names are visible in several places. Have students wear name tags for at least a few days.

- **Class books.** Making class books with a page devoted to each child is a great way to teach names, build community, and let students practice their reading skills. You could make new versions of books (for example, Merle Peek's *Mary Wore Her Red Dress and Henry Wore His Green Sneakers* or Audrey Wood's *Quick as a Cricket*) by letting each child write and illustrate a page from the book.

- **Other academic activities.** Graph class names from shortest to longest. Put all of the children's names in a pocket chart and sort according to sounds or phonetic parts they have in common. Rewrite familiar nursery rhymes to include the names of children in the class (make sure students are comfortable with these rhymes and take them in the playful manner intended).

Other ways to help first graders learn each other's names and feel the power of friendly greetings include:

■ **Making a game of it.** Engage students in a variety of activities requiring the use or reading of others' names. (See the box, "Ideas for Learning Names," on page 59.)

■ **Doing chants often.** First graders love rhymes, songs, and chants, so use these as greetings and ways to practice names. They can range from the simple "We like _____, yes we do! We like _____. Woo-woo-woo!" to more complex chants.

■ **Modeling new greetings.** Show first graders exactly what a warm and friendly greeting between two people looks and sounds like by using Interactive Modeling (see opposite page). Make sure students understand that when two of their classmates are greeting each other, their job is to honor the greeting by giving their full attention to the greeters.

■ **Scaffolding for success.** First graders may need a while to learn each other's names and master the basics of greetings. But once they're consistently showing basic skills such as friendly faces and voices, start adding variations and complexities to this daily piece of your schedule.

■ **Having children say good-byes.** Children can also practice each other's names and the same skills used in greetings by occasionally saying good-byes to each other in a closing circle.

Interactive Modeling of Greetings

Steps to Follow	Might Sound and Look Like
1 Say what you will model and why.	"One of our class rules is 'Be friendly to everyone.' Today, I'm going to greet each of you in a friendly way and you'll have a chance to practice greeting me back in the same friendly way. Watch and see what I do as I greet Anthony."
2 Model the behavior.	"Good morning, Anthony." Use a friendly tone, show a friendly face, and turn your body so you're facing the student.
3 Ask students what they noticed.	"What did you see me do when I greeted Anthony?" (If necessary, follow up with questions such as "What kind of voice did I use?" or "What did you notice about my body?" to prompt children to list the important elements: friendly voice, friendly face, body turned to the person, used his name, and so on.)
4 Invite one or more students to model.	"Now Anthony is going to greet me back in the same way. Watch and see what he does."
5 Again, ask students what they noticed.	"What did you see Anthony do to greet me in a friendly way?"
6 Have all students practice.	"Now we're all going to practice. I'm going to come around the circle and greet each of you. I'll be watching and seeing you do all the things we just talked about."
7 Provide feedback.	"As I went around the circle, most of you smiled at me, had friendly eyes, and called me by name. Tomorrow we'll try greeting each other again."

Good Greetings in First Grade

Beginning of Year	Middle to End of Year
Focus on the basics of greeting (for example, turn body toward each other and show friendly face).	Vary greetings so that students are still practicing the basics but also trying more complex greetings.

- **Teacher greetings.** Greet students individually around the circle, modeling correct name pronunciation, appropriate voice and facial expressions, and so on.

- **Around-the-circle simple greetings.** Pass a friendly "good morning" or "hello" around the circle with no handshake or other body contact.

- **Greeting assigned partners.** Have students pull names from a bag. Or make pairs of numbered cards (two 1s, two 2s, etc.) and have students draw cards. Children with the same number greet each other.

- **Chant greetings.** First graders respond especially well to these. Here's one chant greeting:

Class: "Hickety, pickety, bumblebee. Won't you say your name for me?"

Student: *(says name)*

Class: "Let's all say it! *(say name)*
Let's all clap it. *(clap and say name)*
Let's all whisper it! *(whisper name)*
Let's turn off our voices and clap it." *(clap out syllables without speaking)*

Continue until all class members have been named.

- **Physical greetings.** Use handshakes, high fives, or fist bumps. Be sure to use Interactive Modeling to teach how to make these physical greetings safe and friendly.

- **More playful greetings.** Use fun ways of varying whom children greet. For instance, roll a die and have students count that number of people and greet the last one. Or let students roll a ball to the person being greeted.

- **More complex chants.** Add chants that require movements or more complex interactions. For instance, students could chant, "Two, four, six eight, who do we appreciate? _____, _____, yay, _____!"

The person being greeted could go stand in the middle of the circle and do some kind of activity (for example, jumping jacks) or give high fives to people's outstretched hands as they say the chant.

Getting to Know Each Other

As often as you can, give first graders opportunities to talk about themselves and share information about what makes them unique. Avoid the traditional "show and tell" structure, which often sparks competition to see who can bring the best or coolest version of the latest fad item. Instead, use structures that keep sharing fun and engaging while teaching students to speak succinctly on more meaningful topics when it's their turn to share and to listen when their classmates are sharing.

Sentence Starters for Sharing

First graders tend to be ramblers, so help them keep their sharing focused by selecting interesting topics and providing a sentence frame (at least early in first grade) to guide their sharing.

- My favorite animal is _____ (could also be a game, sport, book, TV show, movie, food, meal, holiday, and so on).

- One thing I like to do at home is _____.

- After school I like to _____.

- I think I am good at _____.

- One thing my family and I like to do is _____.

- One thing I did this weekend was _____.

- My favorite thing about school so far is _____.

- My favorite place to be is _____.

- A super power I wish I had is _____.

- A person I would like to meet is _____.

Use Interactive Modeling to show first graders how to use the sentence frames and speak at an appropriate length on a topic.

Structures for Sharing

STRUCTURES FOR EARLY IN THE YEAR

■ **Around-the-circle sharing.** Each child shares by using the sentence frame with one brief idea to finish it, saying a complete sentence, speaking clearly, and looking at classmates. Build in structures to help students listen and remember what others share. For instance, ask students to listen for connections among classmates by asking questions such as "Who heard someone who likes the same color you do?"

■ **Class books.** Create class books that provide a brief biography of each student. For instance, you could read *I Like Me* by Nancy Carlson or *The Important Book* by Margaret Wise Brown and have students write their own page, listing and illustrating a few things that they think are important about themselves.

■ **Parts of a whole.** Students write something important about themselves on a quilt square or a puzzle piece, and the squares or pieces are combined and posted on the wall for all to see.

■ **Object shares.** Students bring an object from home that shows something about themselves—a family photo, a book they like to read with their families, a birthday photo, or a baby picture. Avoid stuffed animals, toys, and objects that could create competitive or jealous feelings. Do around-the-circle shares where everyone shares their favorite object, or let a few people share each day.

STRUCTURES FOR LATER IN THE YEAR

■ **More detailed sharing.** Each day, one to three children share a detailed interest or a story from home. You could assign topics or brainstorm with students general topics that would be appropriate for school—for instance, things that they do with their families, events involving their siblings or pets, things they're learning to do, or funny moments. First graders may need some guidance as to how to stay brief with these extended shares. Here are a few ideas:

64

- ❖ Model talking about the main idea and giving some details. For instance: "One thing I love to do with my family is make tamales with my grandmother. She learned how to make them from her grandmother. My job is to lay out the corn husks and put meat on the masa dough."
- ❖ Make the "main idea plus details" structure concrete by representing the main idea with one color block such as a Lego or Unifix cube and the details with two different, smaller color blocks.
- ❖ Use sentence frames. "This weekend I went to _____. I went with _____. We had a _____ time because _____."

■ **Writing assignments.** Have students write about themselves, their families, or their interests. Then share their writing aloud. Because first graders are often not fluent readers, their classmates will pay better attention and learn more if you read what they wrote.

STRUCTURES FOR THE WHOLE YEAR

■ **Two Sides.** Give students a series of questions with two choices of answers—"Would you rather eat a banana or an apple?" Divide the circle in half and designate one half for each answer. Students physically move to the half that represents their answer.

■ **Take One Step Forward.** Students stand in a circle. You make a statement such as "I like to go to art class." Students who agree with that statement take one step forward. Everyone takes a moment to see who else stepped forward and then the students who stepped out step back to join the circle.

■ **Clap If You Like . . .** Play some music. Stop it and then call out a physical movement followed by an "if" statement. For instance: "Clap if you like apples." "Stomp if you like bananas." "Dance if you like carrots." After each statement, direct students to watch and see who moves.

See Chapter 4, "Classroom Games, Special Projects, and Field Trips," starting on page 81, for resources that will help you learn more about these and other classroom games.

Model How to Share Information

Interactive Modeling will help students succeed with sharing information with the group or a partner. Be sure to model:

- How much information to share

- What kind of information to share (see "Keeping Sharing Safe for Everyone" below)

- How loudly to speak

- What facial expressions and body language to use while sharing

- What good listening looks like (for example, turning toward the speaker and occasionally nodding)

> **Interactive Modeling**
>
> See Chapter 2, "Schedules and Routines," pages 38–43, for a full explanation of Interactive Modeling.

Keeping Sharing Safe for Everyone

Students often need our help recognizing what news is appropriate for sharing and what should be kept private or shared only with a teacher. Ideas for giving this help:

- **Brainstorm appropriate topics with students.** Post the list.

- **Give examples of private and public information.** Private: "My brother had an argument with my mom about homework." Public: "My brother and I made up a new game together."

- **Have students check with you first if they're unsure.** Tell students if they're ever unsure whether something should be shared, they should run it by you first.

- **Check in with sharers.** Consider briefly checking in with the day's scheduled sharers to find out what they're planning to share. If a topic is inappropriate, review what the class discussed about privacy and help the child find a satisfying alternative topic.

- **Enlist parents' help.** Explain the goals of sharing. Let parents know that if the family has any unsettling news, they should talk with their child about sharing it only with you.

■ React calmly if a student does share something inappropriate. This sometimes happens despite our best efforts. Stop the sharing calmly, try not to embarrass the student, and move on. For instance: "Sean, that sounds like something you and I should discuss privately. You and I will talk, and then you can share about it or something else later."

Learn More About Sharing at
www.responsiveclassroom.org

The Morning Meeting Book, 2nd ed., by Roxann Kriete and Carol Davis (Center for Responsive Schools, 2014).

Class Celebrations

First graders were made to celebrate—in general, they love surprises, parties, and events of any kind. Celebrations can be a special way to build community, bring the class together around a particular event or learning project, and create special memories that foster a love of learning.

However, celebrations can also be problematic for first graders. Sometimes the build-up to events so excites them that they have trouble concentrating for days beforehand. At other times, they have unrealistic expectations. The best first grade celebrations will be those for which you choose themes carefully and prepare thoughtfully.

What to Celebrate

Given the scarcity of time at school, be thoughtful about why you're having a celebration. Some appropriate reasons include helping students learn more about a given topic, showcasing skills or knowledge that students are developing, generating excitement about a given subject area or its potential, or keeping families informed about the progress students are making. Celebrations that are tied to the curriculum in these ways create special memories for students while making good use of their school time.

Tips for Successful Celebrations

■ **Clearly communicate the purpose to students and parent helpers.** Whether it's to showcase skills students are learning or to generate excitement about an upcoming unit, clarifying the purpose of a celebration to students, parents, and any classroom helpers will help the event go smoothly.

■ **Help students have appropriate expectations.** Explain to students what they will be doing at a given celebration, what to expect in terms of treats or special guests, or, if it's an event that they may have experienced before, how it may or may not be the same as "last year's."

■ **Keep it simple.** First graders can become overwhelmed by big events. Extra flourishes are not necessary and might even interfere with the purposes you established, so keep things simple. For instance, a celebration of the author and illustrator Ezra Jack Keats's birthday might involve reading the book *Pet Show*, having all the children write about and do an illustration showing a pet they might want, and then having a "show" of the illustrated pets.

■ **Give parent volunteers appropriate jobs.** If a celebration requires parents or other adult helpers, give them jobs that don't involve content instruction. Also, if some families cannot come, try to involve them in some other way. For instance, if you're having an author party and a child's parent cannot come, invite that parent to visit the classroom earlier, read their child's writing, and leave the child a note.

Ideas for Celebrations	
Area	**Possible Celebrations**
Social studies/ science	**Science day or hour.** Students experience the joy of science in some special way. For instance, students could go on a "science scavenger hunt" and look for a list of items in nature. Or students could have science stations and do an interesting science experiment at each one.
	End of unit party. Children commemorate the end of a social studies or science unit by demonstrating some skill or knowledge they learned or by putting skills and knowledge to work in a special way. For instance, at the end of a unit on balls and ramps, invite parents in to help students use cardboard tubes, blocks, and tape to create machines through which balls and marbles can pass.

Area	Possible Celebrations
Language arts	**Publishing party.** Students share their published pieces with families, other classes, or younger students. **Author birthdays.** Get a calendar of children's authors and celebrate various birthdays by reading a book or series of books the author wrote and finding out what makes (or made) that author special. **Readers' theater performances.** Break students into small groups, each of which practices readers' theater scripts. Invite families, other classes, or selected teachers and staff to watch the performances. **Theme or genre party.** If students have thematic units for reading or genre studies, celebrate the learning at the end in some special way. For instance, to mark the end of a unit in which children read books about animals, students could invite families to join them to read some favorite animal books together.
Math	**___ day of school celebrations.** Although first graders traditionally celebrate the 100th day of school, classes can celebrate some of the other landmark days and numbers along the way—10th day, 25th day, 50th day, and so on, with activities to mark each number. **Game day or hour.** Children play games (especially board games) that get them practicing math skills in a fun and meaningful way. **End of unit party.** Students celebrate the end of a math unit by commemorating the highlights of that unit in a certain way. For instance, at the end of a unit on money, children could have a "yard sale" party where they use play money to buy things classmates have made, found, or brought from home.
Social curriculum	**Friendship celebrations.** Periodically, have celebrations focused on what it takes to be a kind and caring friend. Read books around the theme, have students prepare and deliver written compliments for classmates (put a system in place to make sure everyone receives thoughtful, meaningful compliments), sing some songs that are favorites in your classroom community, or play some games that you've enjoyed together. **Student birthdays.** First graders often enjoy celebrating each other's birthdays. You could have a list with a variety of birthday songs and sing these throughout the day when the children need a movement break. Or you could invite someone from a child's family to come share one of the child's favorite books with the class. If you don't regularly have lunch with your class, it can also be fun for you to join a child at lunch on his or her birthday. (You may want to ask parents of children who have birthdays in the summer, or who don't celebrate birthdays, if you can choose a day at random to give them the spotlight.)

69

What About Holidays?

Celebrating certain traditional holidays at school raises some problems that can be particularly thorny in first grade. First graders often get quite excited about upcoming holidays, and having a school event on top of events their family may be planning can bring their energy to a level that is not productive at school. In addition, traditional holiday celebrations can be uncomfortable for students and families who do not celebrate these times of the year. Finally, most of these holiday celebrations have little tie-in to the curriculum.

However, if you are required to have these celebrations, here are some ideas to make them inclusive and successful:

■ **Halloween.** Have students dress up like favorite book characters. Or have them come as something they've been studying in science—for instance, a planet of their choice—or as a character from a historical period they've studied. Math also presents dress-up opportunities. Students could come as shapes. They could even represent an operation (for instance, for 4 + 2, a student could have four stripes on one sleeve, a plus sign in the middle of the shirt, and two stripes on the other sleeve). Be prepared to help students who might not have home support for costumes, or enlist your art or after-school colleagues to help.

■ **Winter holidays.** Have a party celebrating the new year. Research how cultures around the world bring in the new year and, if appropriate, use some of those customs in your classroom. Or broaden the celebration to include many winter holidays celebrated around the world. With parents' help, have learning stations for several different holidays. The class could also do a service project such as a toy drive or food collection.

■ Valentine's Day. As a class, choose a set of recipients for some extra "love" in the form of Valentine's cards and letters. For instance, students could make cards for another class, the school's custodians, the cafeteria staff, or residents of a local nursing home or homeless shelter.

Recess

First graders love the freedom, movement, and excitement that recess can offer. Playing games together, running around the playground, jumping rope, or sharing knock-knock jokes in the sandbox are all great ways for them to form and maintain friendships and feel like a community. First graders often approach recess with a particular joy that can make it a delightful time of day.

But without some adult guidance, first graders can also encounter problems at recess. Trying to negotiate friendship issues can be challenging for these children as they figure out how to include their many friends in play ("I wanted to play with Rosie, but she was already playing with Elizabeth!") or how to respond when someone else tells them what to do at recess ("I didn't want to swing today, but Noah said I had to!"). It's also hard for them to do even simple things such as running without getting caught up in who wins or loses or who is best or worst at something.

Recess works best for first graders when we carefully introduce and teach the skills required, support students with careful supervision, follow through on issues that arise, and give positive reinforcement of what they're doing well.

Advocate for Different Types of Play

If possible, make sure students have several options for how to spend their time at recess. Some first graders enjoy playing on playground structures. Others prefer "sidewalk" activities such as jumping rope, playing hopscotch, drawing with sidewalk chalk or paint, or blowing bubbles. Many first graders also love to play imagination-based games at recess and will benefit from having an open area for these games.

Teach Recess Behaviors

To be successful at recess, children need us to carefully teach them appropriate recess behaviors. Plan on teaching several brief sessions a day during the first few weeks of school. Start with a quick basic lesson in the classroom about why we have recess and about any recess or playground rules your school may have. Then move outdoors and play a quick whole-class game such as a simple tag game to "practice" these rules. This teaching and practice will demonstrate to children your expectation that they need to show the same kindness and friendliness outside that they do inside. Also model basic recess skills and behaviors such as:

- Getting an adult's attention

- Helping someone who's hurt

- Circling up to hear further instructions about a game

- Getting permission to go to the bathroom

- Staying within play area boundaries

- Responding to the lining-up signal

- Coming back into the building

Keeping Tag Games Safe for Everyone

Model and give students time to practice several key skills to make sure tag games are safe for all:

- **Where and how to tag.** A good rule of thumb is to tag only on the back between the shoulders and hips. A tag should feel firm but gentle.

- **Avoiding collisions.** Model how to watch out for others and keep a safe distance (arm's length) from them as you move about and try to avoid getting tagged.

- **Tagger's choice.** Make sure students understand that if the person tagging believes he or she has tagged someone else, that person has to freeze even if she or he disagrees.

Stop the games at the earliest sign that students are getting rough and repractice these key skills. If just one student has trouble with any of these skills, have that student take a break from the game. At a later point, review and practice the expectations with that student.

Introduce Recess Choices

After those initial lessons, slowly begin to introduce other recess choices and model what they look like. Spend a day or several days with all students experiencing each choice and the ground rules for it. This way, students will fully understand the rules and expectations for each. Teach and model how to:

- Make a recess choice

- Use particular structures (for example, swings and slides)

- Get and put away equipment

- Ask someone to play with you

- Join a game already in progress

- Resolve a problem you're having with someone (see the box "First Grade Conflicts")

Observe and Support

Once recess is up and running, you'll still want to keep tabs on this important part of the school day. Talk to the recess aides and your students, and visit recess occasionally yourself to find out how students are doing. Make sure you provide positive feedback to the class about what's going well at recess.

Also be alert for students who may need further support. Look out for:

- **Children playing alone.** Some children enjoy playing alone, but if it seems a child is not doing so by choice, be ready to intervene. With the child's permission, assign a series of recess buddies, and check to see how things are going. Or spend a few days running large-group games and ask the child to join in.

First Grade Conflicts

Friendship issues frequently lead to conflicts during first grade recess. Here are some things you can do to help students prevent conflicts and resolve them if they occur:

- **Be proactive.** Teach students the difference between issues that are worth doing something about and those that are not. Sort through various scenarios as "little" or "big" issues.

- **Teach conflict resolution.** Teach first graders an age-appropriate conflict resolution technique. See *Solving Thorny Behavior Problems: How Teachers and Students Can Work Together* by Caltha Crowe (Center for Responsive Schools, 2009), Chapter 3, available at www.responsiveclassroom.org. Be ready to guide students in using the technique for a while before allowing them to use it independently.

- **Skip the "no tattling" rule.** Students need to know that when they have a problem, adults can help. You may want to do some teaching and coaching about which issues to report and which to live with, but having a blanket "no tattling" policy allows problems to fester and some students to dominate others.

■ **Exclusionary play.** First graders often experiment with power, and one tool they try out is excluding others. Be on the lookout for exclusionary play and be ready to help students who are excluding others learn to be more inclusive. Help students who are excluded speak up for themselves.

■ **Bullying.** Many first graders tend to be bossy, but sometimes bossiness crosses the line into bullying or other mean behavior. Catching these sorts of behaviors early is crucial to keeping school a safe learning environment.

Play With Students

First graders often love their teachers, and they're thrilled when you occasionally play with them. Pushing trios of them on the tire swing and being one of the jump rope twirlers will provide opportunities to interact with students and find out about them in fun and relaxed ways. Being outside with students gives you a chance to model fun, friendly behavior and helps you keep in touch with what's going well and where children need further support.

Ask for Student Feedback and Check In With Students

Even if you don't have time to go outside for recess, check in with students after recess to see how it's been going. You can do this individually and privately as students enter the classroom ("When we get to the room, whisper to me whether your recess was fun or not so fun.") or wait until all the children are settled in the room and ask for a thumbs-up/thumbs-down signal. You can also have class meetings in which you ask some broad open-ended questions: "What has made recess fun for you so far?" "What do you need more help with at recess?"

Lunchtime

First graders love to eat almost as much as they love to play, so lunch can be a highlight of their day. Lunchtime provides some unstructured social time that gives first graders a great outlet for their talkativeness. But these children will need your help to know how to channel their energy so they can get through the lunch line safely and without too many spills, sit and eat at tables, and clean up in a timely and safe way.

Teach Lunchtime Behaviors

As with every other aspect of the day, first graders need to have all the parts of lunch broken down into manageable pieces. In fact, given how many other things I have to teach early in the year and how complex lunch can

be for first graders, I often try to have students eat lunch in the classroom for the first few days of school. Students either bring their lunches or the cafeteria delivers them. We eat at our desks and begin discussing ways to make lunch work.

Later, we visit the cafeteria to practice how to have lunch there. I model how to go through the line, including how to hold and be careful with the tray, choose food quickly, treat the cafeteria staff with kindness and respect, and many other behaviors. The students practice and, as always, I try to make this practice fun—they pretend they're eating their favorite foods and act out their lunchroom conversations. When we practice lining up quietly after lunch, I close my eyes and see if they can line up without my hearing them. They delight in the shock I express to find them in a straight line in front of me!

Behaviors and skills to teach:

■ Lining up for food

■ Handling the tray, plate, utensils, drink, and so on

■ Making selections quickly and sticking to the choices you make

■ Paying or using a ticket system

■ Responding to the signal for attention

■ Staying in your seat

■ Using basic table manners (for example, keep food on tray and chew with mouth closed)

■ Signaling a need to use the bathroom

■ Throwing away trash

■ Handling spills and cleaning tables and floors

■ Lining up for dismissal

Assign Seats or Tables

First grade lunch works best when students don't have to worry whether they'll have someone to sit with or how to choose among a variety of friends who want to sit with them. Some easy ways to assign seats or tables include making table groups for the week (and placing "name tents" on the tables), assigning lunch buddies, or having students sit with the same people they're currently sitting with in the classroom.

Teach Conversation Skills

Although avid conversationalists, first graders still have a great deal to learn about the art of conversation. They'll benefit from your devoting some classroom or lunchroom time to various aspects of conversation. Some tips:

■ **Teach appropriate lunchtime topics.** First graders need some explicit guidance about the sorts of topics that are appropriate for lunch and those that are best saved for other times of day (like private plans they have with friends, the gross thing their little brothers ate for dinner last night, or a detailed description of their cold symptoms). A sample list of appropriate topics might look like this:

  ❖ Siblings

  ❖ Family events or pets

  ❖ Sports

  ❖ Activities outside of school

  ❖ TV shows, movies, or books

  ❖ Games you play at recess

  ❖ Favorite foods

■ **Model turn-taking in conversation.** Once you have a list, choose a few topics and use Interactive Modeling to demonstrate the give and take of conversation around those topics. If you can, use another adult or older student for this Interactive Modeling. If that's not possible, ask one of your students to help out, but practice with that student before modeling for the class.

■ **Practice and give positive feedback.** Partner students up and have them practice conversation skills such as taking turns talking and listening, making kind remarks, using friendly faces, and sticking to the topic. Be ready to give positive feedback for these important behaviors.

■ **Check in occasionally.** Follow up on your teaching by checking in with students. If you eat lunch with your class, take a few minutes to walk around and specifically notice conversation positives. Occasionally assign a lunchtime conversation topic and check in with students to see what they learned about their partner with regard to that topic.

Eat With Students

In the hustle and bustle of your schedule, it may be hard, but try, when you can, to go to lunch with students. This will give you an idea of what parts of lunch are going well, what parts may need some additional teaching, and who may need some additional individual support around some aspects of lunch. Students will also be happy to have a few extra minutes with you!

Plan a Calm and Quiet Ending to Lunch

First grade lunch is often boisterous and loud. Help students make the transition back to the classroom by taking the energy level down during the last few minutes of lunch. You (or another lunchroom adult if you don't go to lunch) can use Interactive Modeling to teach this routine:

- Use the signal for attention and let students know that they have five minutes left.

- Let students know that during the last five minutes they should focus on finishing their eating and getting ready to go back to the classroom.

- Let them know that the noise level should come down. (You'll need to model what this sounds like—students often find it quite entertaining practicing going from high to low.)

- At your signal, designated tables begin discarding their trash and either returning to their seats or lining up.

Closing Thoughts

Building a strong bond of community among first graders will help every aspect of the day go more smoothly and will help them naturally manage the high energy they bring to school. It's very powerful for the children to see you value each member of the class, establish expectations for knowing everyone's name and greeting everyone in a kind and friendly way, and work to make social times such as class celebrations, recess, and lunch successful. The effort you put into these aspects of the day will reap multiple rewards: Students will likely act with more kindness, respect, interest, and inclusion of others throughout the day.

CHAPTER 4

Classroom Games, Special Projects, and Field Trips

First graders learn best in active and interactive ways. They're happiest and most engaged—and therefore learning the most—when they're moving, singing, and doing. Moreover, when they're doing these things with their classmates, their sense of connection to each other and feelings of community grow. It's not just fun, but essential, for first graders to play games together, do special curricular projects, and go on field trips within or outside of the school.

These special events can create memories for a lifetime. One year my first grade class was assigned the country of Russia for our school's "cultural festival." After reading about and seeing pictures of famous places in Russia, they were most taken with St. Basil's Cathedral and its amazing "onion domes," vibrant colors, and history. So the art teacher and I collaborated on a project. In art class, she helped the students design a large mosaic of St. Basil's with a detailed border around it. On the border, students added small pictures of Russia-related things they had learned about, including matryoshka dolls and beets. She divided up the design so that each student tiled a small portion.

I had never seen students so engaged and focused. The result was amazing, and these students, who are now past elementary school age, still remember and love to go see their creation, which hangs in the school office.

Of course, all projects don't have to be this big. What's important is to infuse first grade life with some games, songs, and activities to make school feel vibrant. In this chapter, I'll suggest ways to do this so that you make the most of first graders' energy and enthusiasm for learning.

Finding Time for Lively Learning

Sometimes teachers worry that games, activities, and special projects take away from academics. But such ways of learning are essential for first graders. Learning and liveliness do not have to be mutually exclusive. Make games, activities, and events purposeful and tie them in to the curriculum as often as possible.

For instance, you can help children learn addition facts by singing math-related songs or work on syllables by clapping the syllables to everyone's names. You could also focus on animal characteristics learned in science by making a class mural to which each child contributes a painting of an animal. It is possible to have fun while focusing on academics!

Classroom Games and Songs

First graders love being playful together. There's a particular feeling of joy and whimsy among first graders earnestly playing a game together, reciting a poem, or singing a beloved song. Being playful together enhances the feeling of community and gives a much-needed outlet for the energy bursting inside many first graders. Here are some tips for making games, singing, and poetry recitations successful:

Foster Cooperation

When first graders are laughing and playing together with no chance of one person being the winner or loser, they can relax and reap the full benefit of whole-class games. They get the message that all of the students contribute and are valuable to the whole class. What follows are a few of my favorite cooperative games to play with first graders.

- **Cooperative Hoops.** Scatter about ten small hoops in the center of the circle. Play some music. When the music stops, students work together so that everyone has part of a foot inside a hoop. Take away hoops so that more and more students have to cooperate to fit everyone in.

- **Hip to Hip.** Play some lively music. When the music stops, children find the person closest to them. You call out a command with body parts such as "knee to toe" and the two partners join those parts of their bodies. Repeat with several rounds of music, new partners, and new commands. You can add in other academics (for instance, when you call out "four plus five," one partner puts up four fingers, the other puts up five, and they figure the sum). Challenge students to make sure everyone finds a partner quickly every time.

■ Movement Chants. First graders love to do chants with accompanying movements. Some favorites are "Oliver Twist," "Tony Chestnut," and "My Bonny Lies Over the Ocean." Once students have mastered the basics of these favorites, they often enjoy doing them in different styles—slow motion, fast, goofy, with eyes closed, in an underwater voice, and so forth.

Work Toward a Common Goal

Competing against each other can be damaging to the class's spirit of cooperation, but you can have them compete together against something separate from themselves. For instance, they could play against the clock or against a stuffed animal or an imaginary friend.

Learn More About Games, Activities, and Energizers at www.responsiveclassroom.org

99 Activities and Greetings: Great for Morning Meeting . . . and other meetings, too! by Melissa Correa-Connolly (Center for Responsive Schools, 2004).

Energizers! 88 Quick Movement Activities That Refresh and Refocus by Susan Lattanzi Roser (Center for Responsive Schools, 2009).

Doing Math in Morning Meeting by Andy Dousis and Margaret Berry Wilson (Center for Responsive Schools, 2010).

Doing Science in Morning Meeting by Lara Webb and Margaret Berry Wilson (Center for Responsive Schools, 2013).

Doing Language Arts in Morning Meeting by Jodie Luongo, Joan Riordan, and Kate Umstatter (Center for Responsive Schools, 2015).

Doing Social Studies in Morning Meeting by Leah Carson and Jane Cofie (Center for Responsive Schools, 2017).

One game students have loved playing in my classroom is "Race to 100" against a stuffed animal. The class has one marker and the stuffed animal another. When it's the class's turn, someone rolls two dice, adds the total, and moves the class marker on a hundreds chart. I help the stuffed animal roll and move its marker. The first to get to one hundred wins.

Another great game is "Bop," in which students stand in a circle holding hands and try to keep a balloon in the air as long as possible without breaking hands or hitting the balloon with a foot or knee.

It might be fine to introduce competitive games later in the year, but limit these to pairs competing against each other. Competitive and sensitive first graders often take losing better when they have a partner to commiserate with!

Be sure to teach what teamwork looks like before introducing games that involve competition, even whole-class competition against an outside opponent. Show children how to support someone who is trying to think of an answer, how quiet cheering sounds, and how to lose—and win—gracefully. Keep everything light and fun, since the purpose of these games is to learn and be playful together.

Choose Active Games

In addition to building community and livening up academics, games help first graders channel their energy in positive ways. Try to find games that require students to move their bodies.

Learn a Small Repertoire of Games and Vary Them

You can learn some basic games and then vary them in infinite ways. First graders usually love the structure of the familiar with a new twist. Here are some examples:

Just Like Me. The simple version of this game is that you or a student says a statement such as "I like dogs." Students who agree with that statement stand up, raise their arms in the air, and say, "Just like me!"

❖ **Coin version.** Give each child a coin. Call out statements that could be true of the coin. ("My coin is worth five cents." "My coin has George Washington on it.") Students whose coins match your statement stand up and say, "Just like me!"

❖ **Animal version.** Give each child a card with a different animal on it. Call out statements that could be true of their animals. ("My animal has fur or hair." "My animal has a backbone.") Students whose cards match your statement stand up and say, "Just like me!"

❖ **Phonics version.** Give each child a flashcard with a word that follows some of the phonics rules they've been learning. Call out statements that could be true of their words. ("My word has a long *a* sound." "My word has the /th/ sound.") Students whose cards match your statement stand up and say, "Just like me!"

I Spy. Adapt the traditional game of "I Spy" in ways that fit your curriculum: "I spy with my little eye a _____ [fill in with shape name]." "I spy with my little eye something that rhymes with _____." "I spy with my little eye a book that was written by _____."

Match Up. Students have cards that can be matched up in a variety of ways. For instance, the cards could show various objects representing three-dimensional shapes. You play some music and they dance around. When the music stops, they find one partner whose card matches their own (cylinder finds cylinder, for example). Other possibilities include matching up cards with rhyming words, equal sums (4 + 1, 3 + 2, 5 + 0), or things in the same categories (animals that are reptiles, animals that are mammals, and so on).

Build in Cool-Downs

Although fast-paced games help first graders expel energy, they often need our help to "come down" from such games. So, when possible, plan for some ways to slow a game down or make it quieter as you get closer to the end. For instance, when singing a song with movement, sing the last rounds slower and slower, then mouth the words silently with action, and finally mouth the words with no motion. You could also teach deep breathing, stretching, or a yoga stance as a transition between games and work time.

Keep Things Fast-Paced and Fun

Explain directions quickly and succinctly, and repeat games often so that the focus of most game time can be on playing, not sitting and listening. Keep the mood light. If a student messes up and another first grader points that out, just give a quick "Oops, those things happen—keep going!" If students are too active, give them a "freeze" signal and let them freeze in exaggerated ways. After they calm down, say something like "Wow, that was fun! Let's catch our breath and try again a little later today."

85

Playing With a Partner

Some games, such as Hip to Hip, require each student to choose a partner. For competitive first graders, this can sometimes turn into bickering and disagreements about who asked whom first.

Especially early in the year, assigning partners yourself or matching students with randomly passed out cards will help cut down on these kinds of arguments.

Slowly Introduce Partner Games

Partner games work well in various curricular areas and can help first graders practice cooperative skills. But you'll need to introduce such games slowly and carefully. Some things to consider:

■ **Teach easy games first.** Start with games with few rules such as Concentration or matching games, so that students can focus on good sportsmanship, turn-taking, and keeping score.

■ **Take the competition out of games at first.** Although first graders can eventually learn to play competitive games in pairs, they first need to practice their game-playing skills with noncompetitive versions. Games such as Concentration and Go Fish can be made noncompetitive by issuing challenges to teams such as "See how many pairs you and your partner can make before the timer goes off." Once you introduce competition, model for children how to be gracious winners and losers, and teach them that sometimes who wins or loses has nothing to do with skill or talent but is just a matter of chance—of where the spinner happens to stop or which numbers happen to come up on the dice.

■ **Reinforce teamwork, cooperation, and sportsmanship.** As students play games, circulate among them and make special note of kind words, turn-taking, focusing on the game, and other behaviors necessary for success with games. When the group comes back together after a game-playing session, share with the class examples of cooperation that you saw: "I heard one partner encouraging her friend who was having a hard time finding matches by saying, 'You can do it. I know you can.' That must have made her friend feel cared for."

> **Great Music for First Graders**
>
> First graders enjoy a wide variety of music, but here are a few artists and CDs I especially love to share with them:
>
> ■ *All Day Long* by Dr. Jean
>
> ■ *Pink Elephants* by Mary LaFleur
>
> ■ *Rocket Ship Beach* by Dan Zanes & Friends
>
> ■ *Down in the Valley* by New England Dancing Masters

Sprinkle Songs, Chants, Energizers, and Poems Throughout the Day

First graders love singing, listening to music, chanting, reciting poems, and doing anything rhythmic. I sometimes think first graders pay attention best when we sing or speak in rhyme. Try singing directions, making up songs to help them remember routines, and doing chants to help them remember academic facts and rules. Consider these tips:

■ **Sing, even if you're not a "good" singer!** You don't have to be a musical person to work music, rhymes, and chants into the classroom. The part of singing that first graders love is joining in, so don't worry about your own musical talents. Seek help from music teachers and colleagues who also sing with their students, or use music CDs or MP3 downloads to give yourself some support.

■ **Choose songs, poems, and chants with lots of repetition and easy-to-remember lyrics.** Singing and chanting will have the most punch if first graders can spend most of their time actually doing these things, not learning long sets of words or movements.

■ **Add movements to help memory.** First graders enjoy adding their own movements to songs and poems, and doing so often helps them remember key lines or words. For instance, one class of first graders decided that for the poem "Way Down South," we should split the group into grasshoppers and elephants to act out the poem in this way:

Way down South where bananas grow, *(All students point to the south.)*

A grasshopper stepped on an elephant's toe. *(Grasshoppers step toward elephants.)*

The elephant said, with tears in his eyes, *(Elephants pretend to cry.)*

"Pick on somebody your own size." *(Elephants point at grasshoppers and say line.)*

■ **Show song lyrics or words to poems.** First graders need to see the connection between the spoken word and printed text. Highlight or have students highlight key words with highlighting tape, highlighters, or different marker colors.

■ **Remember that there is no such thing as too silly in first grade.** When it comes to choosing songs, chants, and poems, remember that first graders love to laugh. Songs or poems about weird or scary events (try Douglas Florian's poem "Beware the Beast"), slightly "naughty" material (try Bruce Lansky's poem "Born Embarrassed"), or nonsense (try Samuel Goodrich's poem "Higglety, Pigglety, Pop!") will be big hits. Also look for songs or poems that the class can play around with, modify, or change altogether (the melody of "Row, Row, Row Your Boat" works for many quick jingles).

87

Special Projects

Many first graders experience an artistic explosion and enjoy all kinds of projects, so it's a great year for weaving artwork and hands-on projects into the curriculum. One year, for example, we studied fairy tales and castles around the world, and students planned, constructed, and painted 3D castles from various-sized cardboard tubes. Remember, though, that first graders have a tendency to bite off more than they can chew, so be careful not to let projects overwhelm them. The following guidelines should help.

Keep Steps Simple

First graders love nothing more than a big, flashy end product—a class book with pop-ups on each page, a brightly colored mural with hidden windows throughout, or a 3D map of the school or playground. But most first graders don't have the planning skills to independently produce the exciting pieces they love. Instead, these projects work best when they can be completed in clear, easy-to-manage steps, or when each child contributes one small piece to a bigger whole.

It often helps to give students an idea of what the finished product will look like and what steps will help them create their own version. You might want to make your own example and then break the process of creating it into chunks. You can display the chunks to help students remember where they're headed and how they'll get there.

Be Sure of Your Learning and Curricular Goals

Be sure each project you choose has a clear role to play in the curriculum and that students understand at a basic level why they're doing what they're doing: "Today we will make game boards that we can use for math, spelling, or phonics. These will also help us with reading and writing because we'll need to add words to our game boards to make the games more interesting and fun."

Include Some Surprises

Most first graders love surprises, so including some element of surprise in projects can be especially exciting for them. For instance, when reading books from a certain series or by a certain author, I've had students write letters to a character of their choice. I'd then write back in the "voice" of those characters and leave the letters in sealed envelopes on their desks. Students are so excited to come into class and find these letters waiting for them. They'll often want to write back immediately!

Give Students Choices When Possible

First grade is often a year of exuberant creativity, and the more open-ended assignments can be to enable expression of that creativity, the better. When first graders have a choice—and some guidance about how to implement their choice—they often are more motivated to learn and show what they learn. For instance, at the end of a unit on plants, first graders could choose to make a plant poster, make a cut-and-paste representation of the parts of a plant, make a 3D model of a plant, or write a story or song about the parts of a plant.

See the section "Class Celebrations" (pages 67–70) in Chapter 3 for ideas of projects to celebrate the end of a unit, an author the class especially enjoys, or a whole curricular area.

Field Trips

First graders generally love special events, and field trips can fulfill both their desire for adventure and their need to have learning come alive in concrete ways. They can explore their love of animals and nature at local wetlands or nature centers, explore their community by going to a fire station or historical landmark, or develop their observational skills by collecting leaves on a hike at a nearby park—the possibilities are endless. Designed well, field trips give first graders a unique view into learning.

Of course, taking a group of young children off school grounds presents some challenges, especially with exuberant first graders. You'll want to take some steps to make sure everyone stays safe, the event meets its learning purposes, and first graders leave as happy as they arrived.

Plan for Active Learning

When it comes to field trips for first graders, think hands-on. Avoid places that mainly offer lectures or other passive learning experiences. Sometimes, even seemingly active trips can fail for first graders if there's not actually anything for them to do but look or walk around! If you can, work with the site to design hands-on learning activities. One of my favorite field trips was to a small art gallery at a local college that featured works by some artists we studied. The gallery allowed children to walk around not with a docent, but with a parent volunteer. With the volunteer's help, first graders completed a scavenger hunt together and then did their own pencil sketch of a painting that caught their fancy.

Obtain Sufficient Adult Supervision

Unless you're staying within your school or walking only a very short distance away, you'll want to have several adults with you. Having extra eyes and hands will help ensure that no one wanders off, children can safely be accompanied to the bathroom, and learning can stay active but appropriate. Be sure to give volunteers guidelines for what you expect on field trips (see "Involving Parents in Events and Activities" in Chapter 5, pages 108–111).

In-School Field Trips

In this time of budget cuts, consider taking some field trips within your own school—to the office, boiler room or other custodial location, the nurse's office, or an older grade's class. For instance, after reading the book *The Little Red Hen* to first graders, my colleague Jean O'Quinn takes them to the school cafeteria. There, the baker shows the class how she will make bread for 600 people, and the cafeteria manager shows them the freezers, pantry, refrigerators, and cooking equipment.

Assign Students to Small Groups Before Leaving School

Think carefully about how to group students for success on field trips, and think carefully about the parent volunteers as well. Who can handle a group of energetic first grade children? Who might need to be with some quieter, less active students? If possible, group students with more challenging behaviors together and lead them around yourself, rather than leaving that to parent volunteers.

Give First Graders a Realistic Picture of What to Expect

Left to their own fabulous imaginations, first graders can conjure up great expectations for a field trip. Be sure to give them a realistic picture of what they will do. Take questions from students so that you can quash any rumors that have been spreading about how they'll get to take home one of the farm animals or jump in the fountain at the state capitol!

Practice What You Can

Practicing the field trip beforehand will also help ensure successful field trip behavior. For instance:

- Practice getting there. Set up chairs in the room like seats on a bus and practice being on the bus together and following bus rules.

- Practice being there. Depending on what you've planned, you could practice how to sit and listen to an introduction, do the activities you've planned, seek permission to go to the bathroom, and thank the field trip leader at the end.

Use Familiar Routines and Procedures

First graders have a tendency to become quite exuberant on field trip days. Following familiar routines and procedures will help keep that excitement manageable. Use the same signals for gaining attention that you would use at school. Closely follow procedures for exiting the classroom calmly. Be sure to hold first graders to typical behavior expectations.

Be Prepared for Some Changes in Behavior

Sometimes first graders seem to change personalities on field trips. Children who are shy and reserved in the classroom become the life of the party during the introductory lecture. Children who are usually outgoing and fearless (and whom you accordingly paired with another adult) cling to you and seem to need your assistance at every turn. So remain flexible. Change children's group assignments if necessary. Take children who are struggling aside, give them a moment to collect themselves, and then together make a plan for what will help them succeed on the field trip.

Make Sure Bathrooms Are Available

I have never been on a first grade field trip without taking at least one student to the bathroom. Be sure the place you're going has bathrooms and know where they are. Send children with adults. You might also want to bring some extra clothes, just in case (see "Bathroom Routines" on pages 46–47).

Think About Food and Water Needs

If first graders are going to be gone on a field trip for much more than an hour, they'll benefit from having a snack and water break. A quick refueling will help them stay focused on the events of the field trip and will help them manage their energy.

If you're going to miss your regularly scheduled lunch, here are some ways to have lunch on the field trip:

- **Collect everyone's lunches before you leave.** Make sure children's names are on their lunches! For students who get lunch from the cafeteria, either have their field trip lunches delivered to your classroom or allow yourself time to pick them up. Place all lunches in a cardboard box or two.

- **Plan where students will eat.** Check with the location where you'll be having the field trip to see if they have enough space for the children to eat at tables. If not, see if you can round up some cloth or paper tablecloths or blankets to take along so that students won't have to eat on the ground.

- **Pack hand sanitizer.** Make sure students use it before eating. You may also want to pack a few napkins, paper towels, or wipes to help students with spills or food on their hands and faces.

Reflect on Field Trip Learning

Help first graders connect their field trip to what they're learning in the classroom. They could write in a journal about what they learned on the field trip or do sketches of what they saw. Or they could each write one page about what they learned, and you could turn those pages into a class book. Students could do follow-up activities or projects—after visiting an art gallery, they could mix paint and dabble in the styles they saw. Writing thank you notes with some detail to the host site can also allow students to practice literacy skills and reflect on learning within a meaningful context.

Closing Thoughts

With the zest for life they bring to school, first graders need the outlet of games, songs, movement, special projects, and field trips. Every day doesn't need to be a party, but try to make learning come alive frequently, and build special moments into each day. Doing so will strengthen your classroom community, help students make much-needed connections between school and the "real world," and foster a love for school and learning.

CHAPTER 5

Communicating With Parents

Fostering supportive, two-way conversations between families and teachers is especially crucial in first grade. This grade often feels like a "big year" for parents—their children are, in many ways, joining the "real world" of school; most learn to read; and all grow and change in many ways. Parents may seek our help—in how to support their child's reading development, for example, or what to do when friendship dramas unfold. Offering support when needed can make a huge difference in their child's life. And we, too, have much to learn from parents about the precious children they entrust to us.

I will never forget the first day of my first year of teaching first grade. It was orientation day, and I had spent all summer preparing the classroom. When the parents and children arrived, I expected joy and maybe some shyness. I was taken aback when more than one parent burst into tears at the sight of the first grade desks and supplies. To them, it seemed their children had grown up overnight!

I was so struck by what a leap of faith it took for these parents to leave their children with me—a virtual stranger and new teacher to boot. It motivated me to do the best I could to educate these children. Memories of those tender reactions carried me through difficult times when I hit bumps in the road in working with parents, reminding me that parents ultimately just want what's best for their child.

In this chapter, I'll share some ideas for how to communicate effectively with families and some suggestions for addressing the particular worries of first grade parents.

About the Term "Parent"

Students come from a variety of homes with a variety of family structures. Many children are being raised by grandparents, siblings, aunts and uncles, and foster families. All of these people are to be honored for devoting their time, attention, and love to raising children. Coming up with one word that encompasses all these caregivers is challenging. For simplicity's sake, this book uses the word "parent" to refer to anyone who is the child's primary caregiver.

Strategies for Good Communication

All communication strategies you use should offer a two-way street between you and parents. Parents know their children better than we ever can, so they have a great deal to offer us. Phone calls home should always include some time for parents to share, letters should always invite responses or feedback from parents, and we should be sure to truly listen even in quick hallway conversations with parents.

Start Reaching Out Early—With Positives!

Communication cannot start early enough—parents need to hear from you as soon as you know their child is in your class. Once you receive your class list, send parents a quick welcome note. Once the school year is under way and you've had a chance to interact with a child, be sure to tell parents about positive qualities their child is exhibiting. Even a quick communication of this sort can make a difference ("Dan really loves information books—he can spend such a long time poring over them and loves sharing details from them with me, especially details about machines!"). Such communication helps build parent trust, communicates to parents that you value their child, and sets the stage for all future communications. You can reach out in many ways:

■ **Introductory letter.** Over the summer or at the start of the year, send parents a brief, friendly letter. Introduce yourself, give them and their child an idea of what first grade will be like, and demonstrate what an exciting year lies ahead. Be sure to invite parents to contact and communicate with you as well.

I also often include a short survey for parents to fill out. I usually ask for contact information and brief information on:
  ❖ Siblings and their ages
  ❖ Pets or special stuffed animals
  ❖ Hobbies or special interests
  ❖ What parents see as their child's strengths
  ❖ What parents would like their child to accomplish in first grade
  ❖ Anything else parents think would be helpful for me to know

Sample Letter to Parents

Dear Parents and Caregivers,

I'm very excited to be teaching your child this year, and I'd like to give you a little information about myself and what first grade will be like. I grew up in a large family in Nashville and live with my dog, Mudge. In my spare time, I like to read, cook, and garden.

First grade is a big year academically. Students learn to read, write on topics in a more extensive way, and do much more complicated math. You will see such exciting growth in your child this year, and I look forward to helping all the children reach their potential.

We have several big themes in first grade. In literacy, we'll explore a variety of authors and series—we'll read books by Ezra Jack Keats, books from the *Mercy Watson* series by Kate DiCamillo, and my favorite, *Henry and Mudge* by Cynthia Rylant. Toward the end of the year, we'll also have a big fairy tale unit in which we'll read a variety of stories from around the world. In science, we will investigate balls and ramps and explore living things as we build aquaria and terraria in our classroom. On the social studies side, we'll explore our local community as well as toys and their history and development. In math, children will be working with larger numbers, furthering their understanding of addition and subtraction, and exploring basic principles of geometry.

In the first days of school, I'll ask the children what they'd like to learn and accomplish in school this year. As a class, we'll then create classroom rules that will enable all class members to fulfill their school hopes and dreams.

I'd love to get to know you and your child by hearing your thoughts. I've attached a short survey for you to fill out. Please return it with your child as soon as you can. I look forward to seeing all of you on Parents' Night, when I'll share more about first grade and answer any questions you might have.

If you'd like to be in touch before then, please call (xxx-xxx-xxx) any day before 8 PM or email me (ms_wilson@school.org) anytime. I look forward to meeting you and hope you continue to enjoy your summer.

■ **Informal classroom visits.** If possible, arrange a time before school starts so that parents and children can come to the classroom, meet you, and see what the room is like. Keep conversations brief and positive, and try to put children and parents at ease as much as possible.

■ **Phone calls and email.** Contact parents early in the year through phone calls or emails. (It often helps to schedule a certain number of students a day until you work your way through your class list.) Keep this initial call as positive as possible—relay a quick story or positive observation: "I have definitely seen the love of music that you told me about in Miranda. Whenever we sing, her face lights up, and she joins in with gusto."

■ **Formal open house ("Parents' Night").** If your school schedules a formal gathering for parents, take advantage of this night to share information with parents about the upcoming year. Display examples of student work and let parents know what a typical day looks like in first grade. Answer parents' general questions, but try not to get into lengthy individual conversations. If parents seem to have particular concerns, schedule a separate time to talk.

■ **Website.** If most families have Internet access, you could have a class website. You can use it to share news about current happenings, post newsletters, and share general information about children's development in first grade. (Be sure to follow your school's or district's guidelines for the use of websites.)

Emailing Parents

In general, serious or confidential matters are best discussed in person, by phone, or in a paper-and-envelope letter. But email can be great for quick notes about day-to-day classroom life. A few things to consider:

■ **Know if parents can—and want to—use email.** At the fall open house, invite parents to sign up to receive email from you if they'd like. Tell them you'll also be communicating in other ways. Judge by the number of sign-ups whether to use email regularly.

■ **Keep the volume of messages manageable by mixing in other ways of communicating.** Most parents rely less on email once they know you'll be sharing news in various ways.

■ **Follow the guidelines.** Check whether your school, district, or parent organization has guidelines for emailing families.

Listen

In every communication with parents, do your best to temporarily put aside what you have to say to truly listen to their views and concerns. Try to keep an open mind, be genuinely curious, and ask open-ended questions if you need more information to understand what they're saying.

Empathize

In every encounter with parents, start with the presumption that all parents want to help their children. For instance, if you describe a problematic behavior and the parent says, "We don't see that at home," avoid arguing or trying to prove that the behavior is happening. Follow up with an inviting, open-ended question: "Tell me about what David is like at home. What do you see?" Even if parents adopt a tone that sounds like an attack, assume it is not. Let the parent finish talking. If you need to, give yourself some thinking time by saying something like, "I've heard what you have to say and would like some time to think about it. Let's talk again tomorrow."

Always try to be empathetic. Put aside your own experiences and judgments and attempt to see issues from parents' points of view. Doing so will help keep the two-way communication line open between parents and you. Many parents are understandably quite sensitive to any communications that feel threatening or judgmental to them.

Communicate Regularly and Consistently

Strive for regular and consistent communication with parents. If parents can contact you, make sure they know your preferred contact methods and times. If you send home a newsletter, send it out on a predictable schedule. If you have a class website, update it regularly. Good topics are updates on what the class has been working on, upcoming plans or events, and ways parents can support children's learning at home.

Occasionally, you may also want to address topics of particular concern to first grade parents, especially those that have been brought to your attention by more than one parent. (See "Special Concerns of First Grade Parents" on page 102.) Address these briefly and reassuringly, and, when possible, offer ideas for what to do at home. There's an example of such a note in the box to the left.

Share Information About Child Development

Many parents appreciate receiving as much helpful information as you can give them about their child. First grade parents may especially worry about whether their children are progressing as they should or how they stack up against other children. Sharing common first grade developmental changes and experiences gives parents a broader perspective.

Here are some points to consider communicating to families about first graders' growth and development:

■ **Children develop at different rates.** Human growth and development is complex, and no two children will reach the same developmental stage at exactly the same time. For example, many first graders are "bossy" and like to test limits with authority figures, but some children are more easygoing and never seem to go through this phase.

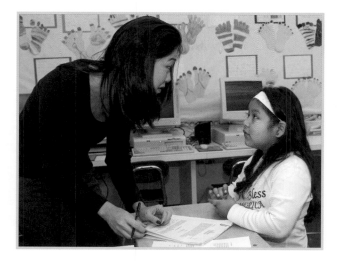

■ **Different aspects of development occur at different rates.** For instance, a first grader might be quite advanced in terms of social skills, showing great empathy for others and amazing conversational skills. That same child, however, may not yet be a fluent reader.

■ **Children will change as the year progresses.** Many first graders begin the year as quite social beings who thrive on human contact, but as they move toward second grade, they may begin to balance this social side with a need to spend more time on their own.

■ **Growth often happens in fits and starts.** Children experience great bursts of growth followed by quieter periods and sometimes revisit behaviors from earlier stages. Some first graders, for instance, experiment with baby talk.

■ **First graders tend to thrive on positive feedback and take even minor criticism to heart.** Let parents know how much specific, positive feedback can help their children. First graders can be equally sensitive to what they see as negative feedback, and parents should be cautious in the tone they use and the words they choose.

■ **Most first graders are very social but also experience some social challenges.** Many often start talking about having "best friends" and play with a variety of people. But first graders can also be competitive. Some vie for particular friends or experiment with bossing friends around.

Child Development Resources for Parents at
www.responsiveclassroom.org

Yardsticks: Child and Adolescent Development Ages 4–14, 4th ed., by Chip Wood (Center for Responsive Schools, 2018), or the child development pamphlets based on this book.

Invite Parents to Get Involved

Let parents know how much you want their support. Many parents would like to be involved in the classroom but are not sure how to volunteer, so be specific about how parents can help the class. Try to find out if parents have any special interests or talents that might be useful. Even if parents don't have specific skills or interests, they can help in numerous ways in the classroom. You'll just need to find ways to guide them. (For more on having parents in the classroom, see "Involving Parents in Events and Activities" on page 108.)

Special Concerns of First Grade Parents

Knowing some of the common worries of first grade parents will let you alleviate parents' concerns and give them strategies for helping their child with issues at home.

Reading

Reading is a pressing concern for many first grade parents. Most students become more experienced readers in first grade— and parents want to see their child make fast progress. If they don't, many start to worry.

Reassure parents by keeping them posted as you see their child making progress with reading. Let them know what they can do to support reading at home:

■ **Make reading times positive.** Let parents know that reading aloud frequently to children is very powerful. Explain that the more positive these read-aloud and other reading experiences are, the more motivated their children will be to read. Also give parents ideas for how to support their child's efforts to figure out unknown words when their children are reading to them.

- **Have a wide variety of books available.** Encourage parents to use the school and public libraries to give their child the opportunity to explore a wide variety of books.

- **Avoid comparisons with other children.** Let parents know that all children learn to read at different rates, and reading early is not necessary to becoming a strong and fluent reader.

Temperament

Some parents of first graders can be caught off guard by changes in their children's personality and energy levels. Parents sometimes question whether the exuberance, high energy, and talkativeness of their children are signs of problems. Or they just find these behaviors a bit challenging at home—they want a little peace and quiet! Of course, if a specific child seems to have attention or other challenges, be ready to discuss those challenges with parents. Otherwise, reassure parents by letting them know that many first graders go through a more talkative, social, and "busy" phase and that eventually their energy level will even out.

> **Support Parents of Children With Diagnosed Reading Disabilities**
>
> Although many first graders just need time to develop reading skills, this is also a year when some students are identified as having specific reading challenges. Help parents of these children get extra support, information, and guidance about working with their children.

Still other first graders begin to test limits at home, and parents may wonder how their children are behaving at school. Again, let parents know that some of this behavior is fairly common from a developmental standpoint. If you can, suggest that setting firm but kind limits will help their children during this period.

Academic Progress

Especially with the increased interest placed on academics in the early grades, some first grade parents worry about their child's progress in this area. Some may question whether the first grade curriculum is challenging enough for their children. Still others may wonder about how they can supplement at home what you're doing at school.

Here are some things you can encourage parents to do to support academic progress in their first graders:

■ **Look for success first.** Sometimes parents are quick to complain about what their children cannot do. Encourage parents to look for what they can do, as it's easier for students to build on their strengths. First graders thrive on this positive feedback.

■ **Give feedback on effort, not on how "smart" the child is.** Many parents attempt to support their children by telling them how smart they are, but these well-intended remarks can be problematic in the long term. Encourage parents instead to focus on students' efforts and connect those efforts to outcomes so that students learn that they can accomplish a great deal by working hard: "You really took your time with that note to Grandma, and your writing turned out so neat and easy to read!"

■ **Keep things in perspective.** Although parents should have high expectations for their children, give them some guidance about what academic expectations are appropriate for this grade. If you see signs that first graders are experiencing stress or nervousness about their academic progress, gently let parents know that perhaps expectations at home are a bit too high and explain that such stress may interfere with a child's progress.

■ **Keep learning fun.** Encourage parents to make learning at home active and fun. For instance, parents can work on math skills when they're out shopping, by playing store with their child at home, or through math games. Children can write in natural ways around the house, including making lists, writing messages on a kitchen chalkboard, or sending emails or letters to friends or relatives.

Homework

If you're required to give homework for first grade students, plan carefully so the children can be successful with this aspect of school. Some of the biggest rifts between parents and teachers can arise over this touchy issue, so take proactive steps to keep your relationship with parents positive. Here are some ideas to help:

■ **Practice at school first.** Give first graders some idea of what homework looks like by practicing for a week or so at school before sending assignments home. Give children some ideas of important habits to consider—having a relatively quiet location, gathering

pencils and any other supplies, what to do if they get "stuck," and where to put their homework so it gets to school the next day.

■ **Be clear about the purpose of homework.** Think carefully about what you want students to gain from homework and share those goals with parents and students. Being clear can keep parents and students from feeling as if homework is just busywork that's interfering with their lives outside of school.

■ **Provide clear homework directions.** Be specific about the homework task and what homework should look like when it's finished. Never assume that the student or parent can figure out the directions for themselves.

■ **Choose tasks first graders can complete successfully by themselves.** Homework goes most smoothly when students can successfully complete the task on their own. If students are going to practice certain skills, make sure that their work at school has prepared them to do so independently at home.

■ **Use homework to practice previously learned lessons.** Homework should reinforce the day's learning. Introducing new concepts in homework assignments may cause confusion and anxiety.

■ **Keep homework short.** Having less homework that students can actually do well and independently is preferable to having more homework that just leads to frustration, boredom, or complaints.

■ **Let students and parents know how to handle homework problems.** Parents may need guidance about what to do if their first grader struggles with homework. If you are comfortable letting parents call you, give that

as an option. Otherwise, let them know that they can write you a note explaining that a problem came up with homework. Both options are preferable to having parents and students muddling through and doing assignments incorrectly or becoming frustrated.

■ **Be sensitive to family difficulties.** Having empathy for the many different home lives of children can help you avert one large source of homework conflict between parents and students or students and teachers. Some students live in circumstances that preclude having necessary materials and a set time, place, and routine for doing homework. Be ready to adjust homework expectations as needed.

Productive Parent-Teacher Conferences

First grade parent-teacher conferences can be joyous affairs, as students often grow by leaps and bounds in first grade and it's exciting to share this growth with parents. These conferences go most smoothly when we follow the same guidelines that govern all communications with parents—approach them with a genuine curiosity about what they have to say, assume the best intentions, and be ready to answer questions.

Come Prepared

Parent-teacher conferences often go much more quickly than we would like. Come ready to make the most of the time by having an outline for each conference. Keep close at hand the student work you would like to show, assessment results, and anything else you want to share.

Highlight the Positives

Be sure to start with the positives and spend at least some conference time exploring what is going well for a child, even a struggling child. If we are looking, we can find strengths and accomplishments to celebrate in all children. Parents need to hear these. Sharing them will help parents put their children's struggles into perspective, develop more positive feelings about school, and be more receptive to ideas, advice, and concerns you may need to share.

Address Concerns Constructively

If you have concerns to share, follow these guidelines to help parents react constructively:

■ **Use neutral, nonjudgmental language.** Describe the behavior you see, rather than relying on labels: "On several occasions, Lewis has become quite upset when problems arise at school; once, he knocked over a chair in frustration when he could not figure out his math assignment," instead of "Lewis has a bad temper."

■ **Present just one or two concerns.** Be honest with parents, but prioritize your concerns and deal with one or at most two related ones at a time. Parents can easily feel discouraged, overwhelmed, or unnecessarily worried when they hear a long list of concerns. And they may feel that you're being too negative about their child.

■ **Have a plan.** Mention what you're already doing to support the child and try to have some ideas ready for how you and the parents can continue offering appropriate support.

A Sample 30-Minute Conference

Five minutes: Opening conversation. Share the plan for the conference and help parents relax. Have a quick, positive, and upbeat story to share, or ask parents some open-ended questions. For instance, if it's the first conference of the year, you might ask, "What did your child like about school last year?" or "What is your child like at home—what does she or he like to do?" In later conferences, you might inquire about some positive developments parents are seeing in their children or what is going well at home.

Ten minutes: Report on behavior progress and concerns. Begin with positives and be as specific as you can in describing what you have seen. If you have areas for concern, share those and invite parents' observations with questions such as "What have you been noticing?" Leave time for any additional ideas or concerns from parents as well.

Ten minutes: Report on academic progress and/or concerns. Again, it's helpful to start with a child's academic strengths, giving as many specifics as possible. Share your concerns and respond to parents' concerns as well.

Five minutes: Closing. Summarize the conference. Make sure parents have time to ask questions or share any other concerns and make plans to check back in together, if appropriate.

Be Prepared for Surprises

No matter how much we plan for conferences, surprises still arise. Sometimes parents raise issues or concerns that you have not previously heard about or considered. Listen with an open mind and let parents know you're considering their comments seriously: "That's interesting. Can you explain more?" If necessary, let parents know that you need more time for a given problem or observation: "Whenever I see them play, Kyle and Morgan are always getting along well, but I'll try to pay closer attention in the next week to see if I notice any of the problems you've raised." Then set a time to talk again.

Follow Up

After conferences are over, be sure to send a note to parents thanking them for the time they shared with you (follow your school's policy on sending notes). If you made any plans with parents for providing support, gathering more information, recommending resources, or involving other professionals, make sure to follow through in a timely manner.

Involving Parents in Events and Activities

First graders often love seeing their parents at school or involved with a special project from home. First grade parents often feel more connected with the class when they have the opportunity to be included. And parent support can often enable you to hold events, plan projects, or be more efficient with your own everyday tasks. These tips can help you be purposeful in your efforts to involve parents:

Set Expectations for Parents

Parents often feel nervous about helping at school. Make volunteering as smooth and easy for them as possible by letting them know what to expect. Be sure to explain exactly what they will be doing. Let them know about classroom rules and behavior expectations as well—first graders can easily become distracted by parents who fail to follow classroom guidelines. Set out explicitly what you expect from parents, as in the sample guidelines shown in the box "Sample Written Guidelines for Parent Volunteers."

Sample Written Guidelines for Parent Volunteers

Thanks for volunteering in our class. It means a great deal to your child and our whole class that you're willing to share your time with us.

Here are some guidelines to help you when you volunteer:

- If you have any questions about what you should be doing in the classroom, feel free to ask me.

- When I ring my chime or raise my hand, it means the students should stop talking and look at me. It helps if other adults in the classroom do the same.

- If you're helping students with a project, try to make sure children do as much of the work as possible, take turns, and help clean up. If you give out materials, have all students keep hands in their laps and wait until everyone has what they need.

- If you're working with a small group, please follow our class rules by speaking to the children respectfully and calmly.

- Most students love working with a parent volunteer, so things will probably go smoothly. But if you're concerned about a child's behavior, please let me know. Feel free to positively redirect children. ("Keep your hands to yourself," "Stay close to me," "Quiet voices.") But if any further steps are needed, please let me handle them.

- If a student should have a problem, please protect that child's privacy by not discussing the issue with others.

Maintain Consistent Discipline

Be sure to hold all students, including those whose parents are volunteering, to your usual expectations with regard to behavior, routines, and how they treat others. Use the same language and consequences with students who need some behavior guidance or redirection as you would if parents were not present. Maintaining the same disciplinary approach will help students and volunteers feel more comfortable.

First graders' behavior sometimes changes because they're so excited to have parent volunteers or visitors in the classroom. Be understanding, but also intervene if appropriate and help the children return to being productive and kind classroom community members. The chart on page 110 shows some typical situations and ways you might respond.

When Children Misbehave During Family Visits

Situation	What You Might Say or Do
Alex's grandmother has come to help students make a background mural for a readers' theater production. Alex is so excited that she talks in a very loud voice and jumps up out of her chair on several occasions.	"Alex, it is very exciting that your grandmother is here. Come sit with me for a few minutes to calm down so that everyone can keep working."
Annie's mother has come to share a favorite picture book. Annie raises her hand and says in a babyish voice, "Mommy, can I sit in your lap?" Her mother gently says, "No," but Annie starts to climb in her lap and say in a pleading voice, "Pleeease."	"Annie, return to your spot. Your mom is here to share the story with everyone." (Go sit beside Annie on the carpet and give her a reassuring nod or smile.)
On a field trip through a local wetlands, Nathan's father is guiding one group. Nathan keeps running ahead of his group to be the first one at each station. He often announces what the group is to "discover" when they arrive.	Speak to Nathan's dad and ask him to keep Nathan with the group. Kindly offer to move Nathan into your group if that would be helpful.

Give Parents Nonteaching Roles

Parents have many talents, experiences, and skills that can benefit the class, but most do not have the expertise to guide first graders through complex tasks like reading or writing. Avoid assigning them tasks that would require special knowledge of how to teach certain subjects—for example, invite parents to be guest readers, but keep the actual reading instruction for yourself.

Family Participation Ideas

School-Day Ideas

- Help with messy or complicated art, science, or other projects
- Chaperone field trips
- Help make books of students' writing
- Share special art, language, or other expertise
- Have lunch with their child
- Do photocopying, stapling, cutting, and other tasks

Evening Ideas

- **End-of-unit celebrations:** Fairy tale plays, readers' theater, presentations of science or social studies projects
- **Reading night or book parties:** Students share projects about books they've read
- **Math games night:** Students teach family members their favorite math games
- **Art gallery openings:** Families view a display of children's artwork

Try to Involve All Parents

Some parents simply are not comfortable with or do not have time for volunteering in the classroom. But all parents can contribute in some way. Some might volunteer to cut things out at home; others might want to contribute supplies for a class party. You may want to have a sign-up sheet on parents' night so that parents can choose ways to contribute. Or, as events arise throughout the year, you may want to reach out to specific parents who might be most comfortable with a particular kind of event. However you do it, be sure to let all students know the ways various families have supported the class so that all children and families feel valued.

Closing Thoughts

Engaging parents in open, two-way communication throughout the school year will set a foundation for both you and them to support and guide first graders through a successful year. Try to set the tone for this communication early and maintain it throughout the year. Parents will appreciate being invited to share their thoughts about their children and their own talents and skills with the class. You, in turn, will learn more about their children and feel more supported as well.

Favorite Books, Board Games, and Websites
for First Graders

In this appendix, I attempt the impossible task of choosing just a few of my favorite books for first graders, as well as some favorite board games and websites. It was tempting just to keep working on this section forever, but it's not intended to be exhaustive—just a start that I hope you find helpful.

Read-Aloud Books

Picture Books

Amos & Boris by William Steig

And Tango Makes Three by Justin Richardson and Peter Parnell

Arf! Beg! Catch! Dogs from A-Z by Henry Horenstein

Bubba and Beau Meet the Relatives by Kathi Appelt, illustrated by Arthur Howard

A Chair for My Mother by Vera B. Williams

Click, Clack, Moo: Cows That Type by Doreen Cronin, illustrated by Betsy Lewin

Duck! Rabbit! by Amy Krouse Rosenthal and Tom Lichtenheld

Fortunately by Remy Charlip

Hattie and the Fox by Mem Fox, illustrated by Patricia Mullins

How I Became a Pirate by Melinda Long, illustrated by David Shannon

I Ain't Gonna Paint No More! by Karen Beaumont, illustrated by David Catrow

I will not ever NEVER eat a tomato by Lauren Child

Jamaica's Find by Juanita Havill, illustrated by Anne Sibley O'Brien

Matthew's Dream by Leo Lionni

Mirandy and Brother Wind by Patricia C. McKissack, illustrated by Jerry Pinkney

Officer Buckle and Gloria by Peggy Rathmann

Olivia by Ian Falconer

Only One by Marc Harshman

Peter's Chair by Ezra Jack Keats

Quick as a Cricket by Audrey Wood, illustrated by Don Wood

113

CONTINUED

Picture Books continued

The Quiet Book by Deborah Underwood, illustrated by Renata Liwska

Ruby's Wish by Shirin Yim Bridges, illustrated by Sophie Blackall

The Stray Dog by Marc Simont

Tacky the Penguin by Helen Lester, illustrated by Lynn Munsinger

The Talking Eggs by Robert D. San Souci, illustrated by Jerry Pinkney

Thunder Cake by Patricia Polacco

Tomorrow's Alphabet by George Shannon, illustrated by Donald Crews

Too Many Tamales by Gary Soto

Tops & Bottoms by Janet Stevens

Traction Man Is Here! by Mini Grey

Two Mrs. Gibsons by Toyomi Igus, illustrated by Daryl Wells

The Wolf's Chicken Stew by Keiko Kasza

Chapter Books

The Castle in the Attic by Elizabeth Winthrop

Clementine by Sara Pennypacker

Gloria's Way by Ann Cameron

Half Magic by Edward Eager

The Miraculous Journey of Edward Tulane by Kate DiCamillo

A Mouse Called Wolf by Dick King-Smith

Nikki & Deja by Karen English

Rip-Roaring Russell by Johanna Hurwitz

Sideways Stories from Wayside School by Louis Sachar

Classroom Library Books

All of the read-alouds I listed are great to stock in the classroom library. In addition, consider these favorite books:

Fiction (All of these are the name of a series or the first book in a series.)

Agapanthus Hum by Joy Cowley

Biscuit by Alyssa Satin Capucilli

Elephant and Piggie by Mo Willems

Frog and Toad Are Friends by Arnold Lobel

Henry and Mudge by Cynthia Rylant

Hopscotch Hill School by Valerie Tripp

Hello Reader published by Cartwheel

Iris and Walter by Elissa Haden Guest

Jackson Friends by Michelle Edwards

Little Bear by Else Holmelund Minarik

Magic Treehouse by Mary Pope Osborne

Mercy Watson by Kate DiCamillo

Mr. Putter & Tabby by Cynthia Rylant

Nate the Great by Marjorie W. Sharmat

Pinky and Rex by James Howe

Poppleton by Cynthia Rylant

Pup and Hound by Susan Hood

Rex and Lilly by Laurie Krasny Brown

Robin Hill School by Margaret McNamara

Poetry

Count Me a Rhyme: Animal Poems by the Numbers by Jane Yolen, illustrated by Jason Stemple

Days Like This: A Collection of Small Poems by Simon James

Flicker Flash by Joan Bransfield Graham, illustrated by Nancy Davis

Kids Pick the Funniest Poems by Bruce Lansky (ed.), illustrated by Stephen Carpenter

Little Dog Poems by Kristine O'Connell George, illustrated by June Otani

Mammalabilia by Douglas Florian

The Random House Book of Poetry for Children by Jack Prelutsky, illustrated by Arnold Lobel

You Read to Me, I'll Read to You by Mary Ann Hoberman, illustrated by Michael Emberley

Informational Texts and Other Nonfiction

A Seed Is Sleepy by Diana Hutts Aston, illustrated by Silvia Long

First the Egg by Laura Vaccaro Seeger

George Washington's Teeth by Deborah Chandra and Madeleine Comora, illustrated by Brock Cole

Ice Cream by Elisha Cooper

I Pledge Allegiance by Bill Martin Jr. and Michael Sampson, illustrated by Chris Raschka

Never Smile at a Monkey: And 17 Other Important Things to Remember by Steve Jenkins

One Tiny Turtle by Nicola Davies, illustrated by Jane Chapman

Red-Eyed Tree Frog by Joy Cowley, illustrated by Nic Bishop

The Reason for a Flower by Ruth Heller

Throw Your Tooth on the Roof: Tooth Traditions from Around the World by Selby Beeler, illustrated by G. Brian Karas

Tornadoes! by Gail Gibbons

To find additional books and authors, talk with other teachers, librarians, parents—and the children themselves.

Board Games and Puzzles

The Allowance Game (Lakeshore)

Blokus (Mattel)

Checkers

Connect 4 (Hasbro)

Dominoes

Fire Station Dalmatian Early Math
Game (Lakeshore)

Floor Puzzles (Melissa & Doug)

I Spy Memory Game (Briarpatch)

Mancala

Sequence for Kids (Jax)

Slamwich (Gamewright)

UNO (Mattel)

Websites

BBC Games ■ WWW.BBC.CO.UK/SCHOOLS/GAMES Contains a variety of interactive games across subject areas.

NCTM Illuminations ■ ILLUMINATIONS.NCTM.ORG Offers a variety of activities and lessons for teaching math; based on the NCTM standards.

PBS Kids ■ PBSKIDS.ORG Offers a variety of educational, interactive games, many of which are based on well-known characters from children's literature.

Reading A–Z ■ WWW.READINGA-Z.COM Contains resources for teachers, including printable leveled books, phonics lessons and worksheets, and assessment resources. Provides limited access for free; requires subscription for full access.

Roy: Tale of a Singing Zebra ■ WWW.ROYTHEZEBRA.COM Contains a variety of interactive reading games and online books, as well as resources for teachers.

Starfall.com ■ WWW.STARFALL.COM Gives children the opportunity to read, hear, and interact with a variety of books for beginning readers.

ACKNOWLEDGMENTS

The first graders I was fortunate to teach over the years deserve much of the credit for any insights I offer in this book. Many thanks to them and their families—they will always be special to me.

I was lucky to teach first grade with two special colleagues—Farrar Richardson and Gail Ackerman. They are both such amazing teachers—full of wisdom, love for their students, and dedication to teaching. The laughter, commiseration, and blind optimism Farrar and I shared during our first year made teaching first grade even more joyful than it already was.

Many other first grade teachers have inspired me and influenced this book directly and indirectly. My own first grade teacher, Miss Bozen, who then became Mrs. Cornelius, made me want to teach. I had the pleasure of watching Marty Kennedy and Debbie Roth teach first grade for many years at University School of Nashville. Marty, Courtney Fox, and Jean O'Quinn shared many ideas and insights with me in the course of writing this book and answered countless random emails patiently and with clarity. Karen Mariano and Christina Glady kindly and generously let me hang out in their classrooms to reconnect with what first graders are like.

Many colleagues at Northeast Foundation for Children supported, guided, and redirected me in the course of writing. [Publisher's note: Northeast Foundation for Children is the former name of Center for Responsive Schools.] Thanks especially to my constant friend and colleague, Babs Freeman-Loftis, and to Mike Anderson and Alice Yang. Michael Lain's editing always makes me sound like a better writer than I am, and Helen Merena's beautiful design made the book itself come alive in ways I could never have imagined.

As always, I also want to thank the people who have helped shape my educational vision and hone my teaching talents—Kathy Woods, who hired me in the first place and still helps keep me on a steady path; Paula Denton, who has always offered a listening ear, wise counsel, and a push when needed; and Lara Webb, who helps me focus, makes me laugh, and helps me stop and appreciate all that I have.

My husband, Andy, knew little about teaching when we married but has made it a point to learn so that he could discuss my successes, challenges, and concerns in a meaningful way. In ways both practical and lofty, he made the book possible. My son, Matthew, always inspires me and makes me want to be an even better educator.

My sister, Helen, has always been especially vocal in supporting my decision to become a teacher and in listening to my teaching escapades. She and her husband, Manny, spent countless hours over the years helping me with various projects, including putting together and gluing hundreds of pieces for Math Their Way boxes my first year. Thanks to my other siblings as well; in so many ways, they've made me the teacher I am.

And, as always, I want to thank my parents. They gave me a love of learning and children. My mom was one of my most loyal classroom volunteers—sewing stuffed animals with first graders, cooking with them, and doing anything else I needed. And my dad is my own personal cheerleader.

ABOUT THE AUTHOR

Margaret Berry Wilson has used the *Responsive Classroom*® approach to teaching since 1998. She worked for fifteen years as a classroom teacher in Nashville, Tennessee, and San Bernardino, California, before becoming a *Responsive Classroom* consultant with Center for Responsive Schools (formerly Northeast Foundation for Children).

Margaret is the author of a number of books published by Center for Responsive Schools, including two other books in the *What Every Teacher Needs to Know* series (kindergarten and second grade), *Doing Math in Morning Meeting: 150 Quick Activities That Connect to Your Curriculum* (with co-author Andy Dousis), and *The Language of Learning: Teaching Students Core Thinking, Listening, and Speaking Skills*. She lives in Riverside, California, with her husband, Andy, and their son, Matthew.

About the *Responsive Classroom*® Approach

All of the recommended practices in this book come from or are consistent with the *Responsive Classroom* approach to teaching—an evidence-based education approach associated with greater teacher effectiveness, higher student achievement, and improved school climate. *Responsive Classroom* practices help educators buid competencies in four interrelated domains: engaging academics, positive community, effective management, and developmentally responsive teaching.

To learn more about the *Responsive Classroom* approach,, see the following resources published by Center from Responsive Schools and available from www.responsiveclassroom.org • 800-360-6332.

119

Morning Meeting: Gather as a whole class each morning to greet each other, share news, and warm up for the day of learning ahead.

The Morning Meeting Book, 2nd ed., by Roxann Kriete and Carol Davis. 2014.

80 Morning Meeting Ideas for Grades K–2 by Susan Lattanzi Roser. 2012.

80 Morning Meeting Ideas for Grades 3–6 by Carol Davis. 2012.

Doing Math in Morning Meeting: 150 Quick Activities That Connect to Your Curriculum by Andy Dousis and Margaret Berry Wilson with an introduction by Roxann Kriete. 2010.

Doing Science in Morning Meeting: 150 Quick Activities That Connect to Your Curriculum by Lara Webb and Margaret Berry Wilson. 2013.

Doing Language Arts in Morning Meeting: 150 Quick Activities That Connect to Your Curriculum by Jodie Luongo, Joan Riordan, and Kate Umsttter. 2015.

Doing Social Studies in Morning Meeting: 150 Quick Activities That Connect to Your Curriculum by Leah Carson and Jane Cofie. 2017.

Morning Meeting Professional Development Kit. 2008.

Foundation-Setting During the First Weeks of School: Take time in the critical first weeks of school to establish expectations, routines, a sense of community, and a positive classroom tone.

The First Six Weeks of School, 2nd ed. From *Responsive Classroom*. 2015.

Positive Teacher Language: Use words and tone as a tool to promote children's active learning, sense of community, and self-discipline.

The Power of Our Words: Teacher Language That Helps Children Learn, 2nd ed., by Paula Denton, EdD. 2014.

Teacher Language for Engaged Learning: 4 Video Study Sessions. 2013.

Teacher Language Professional Development Kit. 2010.

Teaching Discipline: Use practical strategies, such as rule creation and positive responses to misbehavior, to promote self-discipline in students and build a safe, calm, and respectful school climate.

Rules in School: Teaching Discipline in the Responsive Classroom, 2nd ed., by Kathryn Brady, Mary Beth Forton, and Deborah Porter. 2011.

Responsive School Discipline: Essentials for Elementary School Leaders by Chip Wood and Babs Freeman-Loftis. 2011.

Teaching Discipline in the Classroom Professional Development Kit. 2011.

Classroom Management: Set up and run a classroom in ways that enable the best possible teaching and learning.

Interactive Modeling: A Powerful Technique for Teaching Children by Margaret Berry Wilson. 2012.

What Every Teacher Needs to Know, K–5 series, by Margaret Berry Wilson and Mike Anderson. 2010–2011. (One book at each grade level.)

Teaching Children to Care: Classroom Management for Ethical and Academic Growth K–8, revised ed., by Ruth Sidney Charney. 2002.

Engaging Academics: Learn tools for effective teaching and making lessons lively, appropriately challenging, and purposeful to help children develop higher levels of motivation, persistence, and mastery of skills and content.

The Joyful Classroom: Practical Ways to Engage and Challenge Students K–6. From *Responsive Classroom*. 2016.

The Language of Learning: Teaching Students Core Thinking, Speaking, and Listening Skills by Margaret Berry Wilson. 2014.

Movement, Games, Songs, and Chants: Sprinkle quick, lively activities throughout the school day to keep students energized, engaged, and alert.

Closing Circles: 50 Activities for Ending the Day in a Positive Way by Dana Januszka and Kristen Vincent. 2012.

99 Activities and Greetings: Great for Morning Meeting . . . and other meetings, too! by Melissa Correa-Connolly. 2004.

Energizers! 88 Quick Movement Activities That Refresh and Refocus, K–6 by Susan Lattanzi Roser. 2009.

Solving Behavior Problems With Children: Engage children in solving their behavior problems so they feel safe, challenged, and invested in changing.

Teasing, Tattling, Defiance and More: Positive Approaches to 10 Common Classroom Behaviors by Margaret Berry Wilson. 2013.

Solving Thorny Behavior Problems: How Teachers and Students Can Work Together by Caltha Crowe. 2009.

Sammy and His Behavior Problems: Stories and Strategies from a Teacher's Year by Caltha Crowe. 2010.

Child Development: Understand children's common physical, social-emotional, cognitive, and language characteristics at each age, and adapt teaching to respond to children's developmental needs.

Yardsticks: Child and Adolescent Development Ages 4–14, 4th ed., by Chip Wood. 2018.

Child Development Pamphlet Series (based on *Yardsticks* by Chip Wood). Available for grades K–8.

Special Area Educators: Explore key *Responsive Classroom* practices adapted for a wide variety of special areas.

Responsive Classroom for Music, Art, PE and Other Special Areas. From *Responsive Classroom.* 2017.

About Child Development

Understanding children's development is crucial to teaching them well. To learn more about child development, see the following resources:

Child and Adolescent Development for Educators by Michael Pressley and Christine McCormick. Guilford Press. 2007. This textbook presents understandable explanations of theories and research about child development and suggests ways to apply those theories and research to classroom teaching.

Child Development, 8th ed., by Laura E. Berk. Pearson Education, Inc. 2009. This textbook summarizes the history and current thinking about child development in easy-to-understand prose. The author outlines the major theories and research and provides practical guidance for teachers.

Child Development Guide by the Center for Development of Human Services, SUNY, Buffalo State College. WWW.BSC-CDHS.ORG/ FOSTERPARENTTRAINING/PDFS/CHILDDEVELGUIDE.PDF. The center presents characteristics of children at each stage of development in an easy-to-use guide for foster parents.

"The Child in the Elementary School" by Frederick C. Howe in *Child Study Journal*, Vol. 23, Issue 4. 1993. The author presents the common characteristics of students at each grade level, identified by observing students and gathering teacher observations.

"How the Brain Learns: Growth Cycles of Brain and Mind" by Kurt W. Fischer and Samuel P. Rose in *Educational Leadership*, Vol. 56: 3, pp. 56–60. November 1998. The authors, who blend the study of child development with neuroscience, summarize their prior work in a format intended for educators. They conclude that "both behavior and the brain change in repeating patterns that seem to involve common growth cycles."

"The Scientist in the Crib: A Conversation with Andrew Meltzoff" by Marcia D'Arcangelo in *Educational Leadership*, Vol. 58: 3, pp. 8–13. November 2000. Written in an interview format, this article dispels myths about child development and explores ways in which research about cognitive development might inform the work of educators.

Yardsticks: Child and Adolescent Development Ages 4–14, 4th ed., by Chip Wood. Center for Responsive Schools. 2018. This highly practical book for teachers and parents offers narratives and easy-to-scan charts of children's common physical, social-emotional, cognitive, and language characteristics at each age from four through fourteen and notes how these growth patterns relate to learning.

Your Child: Emotional, Behavioral, and Cognitive Development from Birth through Preadolescence by AACAP (American Academy of Child and Adolescent Psychiatry) and David Pruitt, MD. Harper Paperbacks. 2000. Intended for parents, this book presents information about children's development and common characteristics at each age, and offers tips for helping children develop appropriately.

Center for Responsive Schools, Inc., a not-for-profit educational organization, is the developer of *Responsive Classroom*®, an evidence-based education approach associated with greater teacher effectiveness, higher student achievement, and improved school climate. Responsive Classroom practices help educators build competencies in four interrelated domains: engaging academics, positive community, effective management, and developmentally response teaching. We offer the following resources for educators:

PROFESSIONAL DEVELOPMENT SERVICES

- Workshops for K–8 educators (locations around the country and internationally)
- On-site consulting services to support implementation
- Resources for site-based study
- Annual conferences for K–8 educators

PUBLICATIONS AND RESOURCES

- Books on a wide variety of *Responsive Classroom* topics
- Professional development kits for school-based study
- Free monthly newsletter
- Extensive library of free articles on our website

FOR DETAILS, CONTACT:

Responsive Classroom®

Center for Responsive Schools, Inc.
85 Avenue A, P.O. Box 718
Turners Falls, Massachusetts 01376-0718

800-360-6332 ■ www.responsiveclassroom.org
info@responsiveclassroom.org

124